on
reading

Proust
on
reading

with *Sesame and Lilies* I: Of Kings' Treasuries
by John Ruskin

edited and translated by Damion Searls

'on'

'on'
Published by Hesperus Press Limited
19 Bulstrode Street, London W1U 2JN
www.hesperuspress.com

'Of Kings' Treasuries' from John Ruskin's *Sesame and Lilies*, first
published 1865
Selections from Proust's translator's preface to Ruskin's *The Bible of Amiens*,
first published 1904
Proust's translation, notes, and preface 'On Reading', first published 1906
This collection first published by Hesperus Press Limited, 2011
Introduction and translation © Damion Searls, 2011
Foreword © Eric Karpeles, 2011

Designed and typeset by Fraser Muggeridge studio

ISBN: 978-1-84391-616-1

Contents

Foreword by Eric Karpeles   vii

Introduction   xi

On Reading
   Translator's Preface to *Sesame and Lilies*   3
Lecture I — Sesame. Of Kings' Treasuries
   by John Ruskin, Notes by Marcel Proust   45
Makeshift Memory   95
Ruskin in Venice   97
Servitude and Freedom   105
Resurrection   107

Biographical note   113

Foreword

Between the writing of *Jean Santeuil* and *A la recherche du temps perdu*, Marcel Proust committed many years to his translations of Ruskin and their accompanying notes and forewords. Ruskin's voice was engaging, personal and accessible: 'May I ask you to consider with me what this idea practically includes?' the eminent Victorian inquired politely about the concept of one's having a 'position in life'. Proust, whose gift as a translator came not from language skills but rather from a profound comprehension of his subject, struggled to make Ruskin's English come alive in French. What we have in Damion Searls's present selection of Proust's prefaces to Ruskin is an almost Wildean farce of accumulated attributions: I am writing a foreword to his translation of Proust's introductions to his own translations of Ruskin. ('I'm sure the programme will be delightful, after a few expurgations', as Lady Bracknell says.)

In a volume called *Sesame and Lilies*, evoking the masculine and feminine, the foremost English cultural critic of his time collected a series of lectures he had given on the opposing natures of man and woman. In these talks, Ruskin expounded upon the virtue of books and the importance of reading as an edifying activity. 'If you do not know the Greek alphabet, learn it', John Ruskin pleaded to his audience, associating classical values and art's moral imperatives. To discriminate between lighter fare – newspapers, fiction, travel diaries – and more substantive literary endeavors, he made the claim that 'a book is essentially not a talking thing, but a written thing'.

As I made my way through this selection, I was struck otherwise. 'Of Kings' Treasuries' from *Sesame and Lilies* seemed to me to be very much 'a talking thing' indeed; how intensely *aural* the experience of reading it proved to be. The resounding voices of Proust and Ruskin can be *heard* as well as read in these pages. And by juxtaposing the English philosopher with his

French disciple, Searls affords us the rare privilege of over-hearing Proust's mind engage with Ruskin in what is tanta-mount to spoken dialogue. From across the divide of 100 years, we hear Proust vocalise clearly and directly: 'Need I add that if I describe this taste, this kind of fetishistic reverence for books as unhealthy and pernicious, it is only relative to the ideal habits of a spirit altogether lacking in faults, one which does not exist; I do so like the physiologists who describe as an organ's normal function something which is hardly ever found in living beings.' In these pages the writer is not hiding behind a scrim of narrative fiction, so our connection to his verbose, complex sensibility feels more immediate, more revealing. Here we find fully realised the voice first developed in *Les plaisirs et les jours*, later to be fructified in *Contre Sainte-Beuve*.

According to Ruskin a book may not be essentially a 'talking thing', yet he put forth the proposition that 'reading is a con-versation'. Proust, however, maintained that 'reading cannot be equated to conversation', insisting that one reads only in a condition of solitude. Meanwhile, reading these comments, I felt he was speaking within earshot, as if I overheard him speaking at a café table next to mine. Despite his insistence upon the necessity of solitude, Proust developed an engaging writing style that is decidedly conversational, nearly chatty. And his voice is not the only one we hear. Proust calls forth other voices in these pages, cuing entries at precise moments from Matthew Arnold, Anatole France, Emerson, Racine, John Stuart Mill, George Eliot, Shakespeare. Passages from the highly colloquial King James Bible are inserted. Proust is like a literary choirmaster, and resembles the humble pianist who sits down to play for Mme Verdurin, causing her to exclaim, *'je crois entendre un orchestre'*.

Much as Proust absorbed *Pelléas* while tuning in his Théâtro-phone broadcast, we too, reading these texts, can make out distinct, rapturous voices. In a felicitous harmony of eye and ear, I felt I was actually listening to what I was reading.

Proust devoted eight years of apprenticeship to the quirky English critic. His intoxication with Ruskin's aesthetic is palpable and the reader feels a renewed sense of the deep debt gratefully incurred. 'There is no better way to discover what you yourself feel than to try and recreate in yourself what a master has felt.' At the same time, reading these pages, one bears witness to the end of the affair. Proust had come under the sway of Whistler, apostle of 'art for art's sake', whose legal battle with Ruskin had forced him to flee London for Paris. (Proust and Ruskin never met. Proust and Whistler met once, in 1897.) The conflicting insights Proust extracted from these two larger-than-life characters needed constructive reconciliation so as to avoid negation, and in a note found in these pages, he articulated a solution to a seemingly intractable standoff of belief systems: '...these opposites may perhaps meet if one extends the two ideas, not all the way to infinity, but to a certain height'. This was just what Proust was to do, eventually coming to understand that between Ruskin and Whistler 'there was only one truth and they both perceived it.'

Having brought to completion the consuming labor of his translations, Proust then began to address the integrity of Ruskin's ultimate accomplishment. He found serious fault and undertook an impassioned dissection of his master's philosophical weaknesses. Then, with the righteousness of a lapsed believer, he generously ascribed Ruskin's failings to 'an essential frailty of the human spirit'. Proust's biographer Tadié succinctly sums up this process of chrysalis as 'a dialectic of influence, which extends from identification to refutation, and from refutation to assimilation'.

Finally, after the give and take of serious analytic criticism, after the protracted immersion in another writer's words, the sleeping novelist was roused. Efficiently, Proust converted much of what he learned from Ruskin into practical, technical information. Reading the notes in these pages, we feel the emergence of the incomparable practitioner-to-be. Proust bristled at Ruskin's disdain for 'wise men' who 'hide their deeper thought', and offered instead his own observations, created his own hierarchy of thinkers. 'The writer of the first rank is one who uses whatever words are dictated to him by an interior necessity, the vision of his thought which he cannot alter in the least.' Flaubert is held high, *Sentimental Education* extolled. We read of those first-rate books and the writers who 'build and perfect the necessary and unique form' where their thoughts 'will be made incarnate'. Proust's notes and prefaces to Ruskin reveal the exacting mind of a literary critic operating from the vantage point of a structural engineer. Responding to 'Of Kings' Treasuries', Proust constructed around Ruskin's text a verbal retaining wall sturdy enough to withstand the assault of his own commentary. Extrapolating architectural details cited in *The Bible of Amiens*, he reconsidered the integral configuration of the novel. In 'On Reading', Proust's preface to *Sesame and Lilies*, we come closest to a recipe for the mortar and bricks that laid the foundation for *A la Recherche du temps perdu:*

> He moves from one idea to the next without any apparent order, but in reality the imagination which conducts them is following its own deep affinities and imposing on it, despite itself, a higher logic, to such an extent that at the end it finds itself to have obeyed a kind of secret plan which, unveiled at the end, retroactively imposes a kind of order on the whole and makes it seem magnificently staged right up to the climax of this final apotheosis.

These reflections on Ruskin's compositional methodology provide us with a foretaste of Proust's understanding of his own forthcoming apotheosis. He would shortly abandon the need to recreate in himself what a master had felt. Instead, he became one.

– *Eric Karpeles, 2011*

Introduction

> I realised that the essential book, the one true book, is one
> that the great writer does not need to invent, in the
> current sense of the word, since it already exists in every
> one of us – he has only to translate it. The task and the
> duty of a writer are those of a translator.

– Remembrance of Things Past: Time Regained

Although many great writers have also been translators –
Borges, Murakami, Singer, Rilke, just to start at the top – there
is perhaps no writer of such stature for whom translation was
as important as it was for Marcel Proust. He spent eight years
immersed in John Ruskin's work and six years translating two
of his books, a discipline which profoundly shaped his art
and style. Ruskin in fact became for Proust in his late twenties
almost exactly what Rodin would be for Rilke in *his* late
twenties: an older mentor whose creativity through submission,
through concrete attention to physical form (Gothic cathedrals,
sculpture), would give the dreamy, frustrated younger artist
the discipline and confidence he needed to construct forms in
words for own his inner world. Even the mottos they drew from
their respective mentors were almost identical: from Ruskin,
'Work while you still have light'; from Rodin, '*Travailler, rien
de travailler.*'

In 1897, Proust (1871–1923) had written close to a thousand
pages of a long novel, *Jean Santeuil*, but found himself unable
to pull the book together.[1] At this time of crisis, he read Robert
de La Sizeranne's article (later a long book) '*Ruskin et la religion
de beauté*'. Although little read today, John Ruskin (1819–1900)
was one of the most influential writers and thinkers of the nine-
teenth century. Even the briefest summary of his many accom-
plishments would overflow the length of this introduction; he

was rather like Henry David Thoreau, William James, and John Singer Sargent rolled into one, and if the combination sounds impossible, even monstrous, it is meant to. Ruskin's death became almost a national day of mourning in England, with hundreds of thousands joining the memorial parade; Proust's short obituary notice of Ruskin began as follows, showing the stature that Ruskin was quite generally granted at the time:

> We feared for Tolstoy's life the other day; this misfortune did not come to pass, but the world has suffered a loss no less great: Ruskin is dead. Nietzsche is mad; Tolstoy and Ibsen seem to be at the end of their careers; Europe is losing, one by one, its great 'spiritual leader [*directeurs de conscience*]'. A leading mind of his time Ruskin certainly was, but he was also its instructor of taste, its initiator into beauty...[2]

Proust abandoned his novel and turned to studying French Gothic architecture, making Ruskinian pilgrimages (as did many art-lovers at the time, before widespread art photography), and

---

1. Jean-Yves Tadié's biography *Marcel Proust: A Life* (1996; Penguin, 2000) is excellent on *Jean Santeuil*'s strengths and weaknesses: 'he was quite able to describe his life and his feelings between the ages of twenty-five and thirty; but he was not capable of giving them an overall structure or any organizational basis. *Jean Santeuil* is neither the story of a life resurrected through memory, nor is it that of a vocational calling: memory and literature are not singled out here; they are merely themes like any others. Finally the sentence structure is tentative and does not have the fine classical style' of his later masterpiece (p. 284). Tadié later says that Proust's translations were what transformed his style, 'impregnating' it with 'the structure of Ruskin's sentences, which were long, rich in incident and imagery, supple and musical, and [influenced by] the King James Bible' (p. 368). Further citations of Tadié, or of others as quoted by Tadié, will be made in the text.
2. 'John Ruskin', in *Contre Sainte-Beuve, précédé de Pastiches et mélanges, et suivi de Essais et articles* (Gallimard: Pléiade Edition, 1971), p. 439; first published 27 January 1900, a week after Ruskin's death.

writing articles on Ruskin. By early 1900, Proust claimed to know Ruskin's *Seven Lamps of Architecture*, *The Bible of Amiens*, *Lectures on Literature and Painting*, *Val d'Arno*, and almost-600-page autobiography *Praeterita* 'by heart' (Tadié 350), and had decided to translate him. First came *The Bible of Amiens*, which Proust called – admittedly, in a pitch to a publisher – 'beautiful, unknown, and original... the finest of Ruskin's works,' and Ruskin's only book 'to do with France, being simultaneously about French history, a French city, and the French Gothic style' (Tadié 391). The 'Bible' in question is the Amiens Cathedral, specifically its West Portal: Ruskin 'reads' it to explicate the lessons 'Our Fathers Have Told Us' (the title of the series Ruskin planned – *The Bible of Amiens* was intended to be the first volume of ten). One of the book's attractions for Proust, I suspect, was precisely that it let architecture become a pleasure of reading, integrated into the booklike – not bookish – interiority of Proust's imagination. (See the passage on p. 101 below, where Proust is reading Ruskin while actually in St Mark's and the different pleasures blend into one; see also the opening of *Remembrance of Things Past*, where the narrator's first waking thought in the whole novel is that he is what he is reading about: a church.) Ruskin 'reads' the architecture of Amiens, and reading, for Proust, because it lets you share another's thought while remaining in solitude, is the unique royal road to the realms within whose exploration is the artist's one true task.[3]

Along with translating *The Bible of Amiens*, Proust added hundreds of footnotes, which often devour the page of Ruskin to which they are ostensibly attached. They are deeply erudite and

3. This is a good place to mention the translation problem posed by the word *esprit* and its related form *spirituelle*. Proust's entire essay hinges on the nature of this interior realm but I could not translate *esprit* consistently: 'spiritual' sometimes sounded too religious, 'intellectual' too academic, 'mental' too cognitive. I have used all these terms, as well as 'inner', '[life] of the mind', and others, and tried to convey in other ways the unity and consistency of Proust's argument.

enormously diligent, and Tadié paints us a wonderful picture of Proust at work, checking quotations and Dutch geography, adding a four-page footnote on Maeterlinck and another note surveying in detail contemporary medicine: 'Proust never stopped gathering information, even at night, and reading things that were "boring and solemn". In this way he acquired the discipline that he knew was necessary (not just for "neuropaths", but for artists)' (450–52). He used these notes to argue against Ruskin's theories and examples, and to develop and explore his own aesthetic principles; more importantly, they gave Proust what he was always looking for in constructing his books: a structure into which he could pour endlessly more material. There is, of course, the ever-accordioning *Remembrance of Things Past*; his first book, *Pleasures and Days*, is made up of more than fifty various shorter pieces, including stories, poems, prose poems, pastiches, eighteenth-century 'characters', art studies and moral reflections (Tadié 252); the only other book he published in his lifetime, *Pastiches et mélanges*, combines nine pastiches of other writers' prose styles (recently published in English, as *The Lemoine Affair*) and eight shorter pieces of drastically different kinds.

Most strikingly, Proust used his notes to provide a personal anthology of passages from Ruskin's other works in order to give the reader a sense of already knowing them. The idea of creating a 'makeshift memory'[4] of Ruskin's oeuvre for the reader seems

4. This crucial term – *mémoire improvisée* in French – has repeatedly been translated into English as 'improvised memory', which I think gets it wrong. As the context (p. 95) makes clear, the connotation is not of spontaneity or creative virtuosity, like a jazz solo, but of being thrown together or hastily whipped up as a partly effective substitute for the real thing; in a draft passage, Proust calls it 'a kind of fake memory [*mémoire factice*], full of the sensations Ruskin has produced' (quoted in *Contre Sainte-Beuve*, Pléiade Edition, p. 723). The English translation 'improvised memory' appears in Jean Autret and Phillip J. Wolfe's translation in *On Reading Ruskin*, p. 6; Euan Cameron's translation of Tadié, p. 357; etc.

a little crazy, but it is key to the importance of these translations for Proust's own art as it 'flashes forth from his own depths' (p. 3, n. 1). Ruskin's work as a whole – discussed in very suggestive terms in footnote 1 to Ruskin's epigraph (p. 45) – provided a grand enough system for Proust to explore how interconnections work: how to create artistic unity, not from mechanistic cross-referencing but with a consistent 'physiognomy' of thought. Footnotes were a way of establishing relationships and plumbing depths, always Proust's method, and for us these notes reveal Proustian reading in action. That is the justification for including so much of Ruskin's text in a book by Proust: Proust made the Ruskin his own, by translating it, annotating it, and reading it.

It seems likely that Proust was ready to return to fiction after *The Bible of Amiens*, but his father died in 1903 and Proust's grief diverted him away from his inward creativity into another translation. He turned to *Sesame and Lilies*, Ruskin's best-selling book in his lifetime out of the 160 he wrote, with over 160,000 copies in print by 1900: a treatise on education, a somewhat back-handed manifesto of women's rights, and, most appealing to Proust and to us today, a hymn to the power of reading. Along with more copious footnotes, Proust added a long preface called 'On Reading', which describes childhood memories of books, meals, bedrooms, and walks along what he would later call Swann's Way. He published the essay three times: in 1905; as the preface to *Sésame et les Lys* in 1906; and again in *Pastiches et mélanges* in 1919 under the title 'Days of Reading'.

His beloved mother would die while Proust was correcting the proofs of *Sesame and Lilies*, in September 1905, and instead of dedicating the second Ruskin translation to her, as the first was dedicated to his father, he systematically went through 'On Reading' and changed all references to his mother to an 'aunt': perhaps, Tadié speculates, because Proust, 'crippled with grief, was only able to write about his mother once he had transformed her into a grandmother [in *Remembrance of Things*

Past], and thus into a fictional character. This is undoubtedly the most mysterious period in an existence that was rich in secrets' (465–66). Proust then wrote: 'I've closed the era of translations, which Maman encouraged, for good. And as for translations of myself, I no longer have the heart' (Tadié 475).[5] He turned down the offer to translate more Ruskin, even *St Mark's Rest* about Venice, because he did not want to die 'without ever having written anything *of his own*' (Tadié 437).

It would take two more years for Proust to recover, but a notebook of 1908 begins to sketch out *Remembrance of Things Past*; at the same time, he was writing an experimental fictional/critical work, *Against Sainte-Beuve*, which alternates between an attack on the nineteenth-century critic and sections of narrative very much like *Swann's Way*; and he engaged in the last major project he would accomplish before embarking on his great novel, the pastiches of other writers mentioned above. A fragment from *Against Sainte-Beuve* begins:

> As soon as I started to read an author I could hear right away, beneath the words, the tune of the song which is always different from the song of every other author... Even if, never having been able to work, I didn't know how to write, I knew very well that I had this ear, more delicate and discriminating than others' ears, which allowed me to write pastiches and pieces in other authors' styles, because once you have the tune the words come by themselves.[6]

These pastiches, then, were acts of active reading: perceiving, distilling, and reconstructing the artistic core, just what he argued for in 'On Reading' (Tadié 505). He later said that these

5. Already he had called translation 'tedious in many ways,' 'not real work' (Tadié 398). In a letter of 1904, after the publication of *La Bible d'Amiens*, he wrote: 'I still have two Ruskins to do and after that I shall try to translate my own poor soul, if it hasn't died in the meantime' (Tadié 433).
6. *Contre Sainte-Beuve*, Pléiade Edition, p. 303.

pastiches were ways of getting other voices out of his way so that he could create his own; it is a very Proustian paradox indeed that translating should turn out to be more writerly than writing.

I should add here a note on Proust's translation methods because Proust was far from fluent in English – by some accounts practically unable to speak it, though he could certainly read it and spent years immersing himself in Ruskin in particular. His mother, and later an English friend Marie Nordlinger (whom Proust was delighted to discover was from Rusholme, where Ruskin had delivered the *Sesame and Lilies* lectures), provided Proust with first drafts in French which Proust then reworked and reworked again, making 'countless' manuscript corrections.[7] From the beginning, many have been skeptical of this process, as though Proust were somehow cheating. Proust himself overheard a nasty comment at the publisher's about how many errors his translation was no doubt going to have, and responded 'I do not claim to know English; I claim to know Ruskin' (Tadié 399). As someone who has translated from languages I read but don't speak, and co-translated from a language I read poorly, I can attest that the process is not as outrageous as it seems: you can tell when you don't understand something and just ask a native speaker to clarify it. What matters is how well you read – in a spiritual, not purely a technical sense – and how well you write in the language you are translating into. In fact, both French and English readers marveled at how well Proust captured Ruskin's meaning and style (Tadié 400, 433). Proust wanted his

7. Tadié 368; Nordlinger from Rusholme: Richard Macksey, introduction to *On Reading Ruskin*, p. xxii, n. 10. Nordlinger is thanked in Proust's first note to *Sesame and Lilies*; he had suggested to her that they sign the contract together and share the royalties, but she refused (Tadié 436). In fact, in the episode mentioned above of Proust reading Ruskin in St Mark's in 1900, it was she who read it with him – 'He was strangely moved and overcome with a kind of ecstasy,' Nordlinger later said; 'by the text,' Tadié adds a little wickedly, 'not by Marie' (Tadié 348).

translations to be vivid and 'faithful like love and like pity' (Tadié 867, n. 5), and he succeeded.

All biographical details aside, 'On Reading', the centerpiece of the present volume, is full-fledged Proust at his best and a work that repays unending attention and love. Its long first section, on childhood reading, marks the first time Proust sees his personal past as a vanished world, and has developed the techniques to bring it back to life. It could almost come straight out of 'Combray', except for its lack of links to Gilberte and Albertine; at one point, he refers to 'the Méséglise way', calling it by the fictional name it would bear in *Remembrance of Things Past*, rather than 'Méréglise', the real place. The section's balanced construction is another perfection, with a framing paragraph that introduces four set pieces, in the dining room, bedroom, park, and bedroom again, taking place in the morning, early afternoon, late afternoon, and night, and ending with the end of the book he is reading and its being shelved away – only to be unexpectedly reopened in the second half of the essay, like the way the past returns in the present. There is, throughout, the systematic imagery which always gives the Proustian world its unified atmosphere, with the whole in all of the parts, 'every sentence, fundamentally, like every other, because they have all been spoken with the unique inflection of a single personality' (p. 34): for example, in the long sentence describing the objects in Proust's bedroom (pp. 9–11), all eight clauses use metaphors connecting the things in the room to springtime flowers, to the church, or to both (flowers on the altar). These are the two dominant features of the world outside the room, and the next sentence in turn mentions that outdoor altars for the holidays (the boy is on vacation) connect him to the church 'with a path of flowers'.[8]

8. E.F.N. Jephcott makes this point in *Proust and Rilke* (London: Chatto & Windus, 1972, p. 191). The same book (pp. 103 ff.) also draws the parallel between Ruskin for Proust and Rodin for Rilke that I made above.

The second half of 'On Reading', after Proust turns back to his task of introducing, analysing, and arguing against Ruskin, is Proust the critic at his most brilliant and Proust the self-analyst at his most revealing. In the transition to the second section, he explicitly says that the first section's 'delays on flowered and winding paths' were intended to lead the reader to re-create in his own mind the psychological act called Reading: Proust's entire mission, as an artist, was always to re-create in the reader's mind what there was in Proust's, and in 'On Reading' you can see him exploring, one after the other, analytically and almost scientifically, various methods for how to do so. His footnote laying out the disparate facts that went into the description of an imagined trip to Holland is as explicit an account of Proust's fictional method, of the way he transforms elements of his lived experience into a composite experience, as he would ever give – at the moment when he is discovering it.

Finally, he ends 'On Reading' with his great theme, re-capturing the past. Compare the despondent conclusion to his first Ruskin preface, just two years earlier, when he had not yet discovered his techniques for recapturing lost time and had at his disposal only

> a memory which does not correspond to the facts... Not being able to reawaken the flames of the past, we want to at least gather its ashes... It is when Ruskin is far from our heart that we translate his books and set out to portray the lineaments of his thought in a faithful image. So perhaps you will not be able to hear the sounds of our faith or our love; perhaps it is only our piety you can perceive here and there, cold and furtive, and busy, like the Theban Virgin, restoring a tomb.[9]

9. Cf. Proust's note 50 (p. 84, n. 50) on the last word of Ruskin's preface to *The Queen of the Air*: Proust ending his preface to *La Bible d'Amiens* with 'tomb' was surely significant.

The contrast with the glorious finale of 'On Reading' could not be greater: there, in a fivefold metaphor, a five-note chord of sublime harmony, Proust equates Dante or Shakespeare's presence in the reader, the columns in the busy Venetian square, Eastern artifacts in the West, the twelfth century in the present, and personal memories of Venice in his present writing, enrapturing them all in seven final adjectives like the seven themes he claimed to find in the last sentence of 'Of Kings' Treasuries'. In a 1904 letter (Tadié 443), Proust described beauty as 'a kind of blending, a transparent unity in which all things, having lost their initial aspect as things, have lined up beside each other in a sort of order, are instilled with the same light and are seen within each other': in 'On Reading', Proust has the depth of experience and discipline of technique to create it.

About the Texts

This book was originally intended to be a full English version of Proust's Ruskin's *Sesame and Lilies*, with all of Ruskin's text and all of Proust's notes as well as Proust's preface 'On Reading'. But the nature of the Hesperus 'On' series has led to a more focused book, which still provides a new encounter with Ruskin's great work, a glimpse into the workshop where Proust developed his techniques for *Remembrance of Things Past*, and a unique example of the translator's creative art. 'On Reading' is given in full; some, but not all, of Proust's notes to *Sesame and Lilies* are included, with notes occasionally abbreviated without comment when not omitted; the other four excerpts on the nature of reading – , 'Makeshift Memory', 'Ruskin in Venice', 'Servitude and Freedom', and 'Resurrection' (titles are supplied by me) – are drawn from Proust's preface to his earlier translation of Ruskin's *The Bible of Amiens*. 'Ruskin in Venice' skips passages after the first sentence, second sentence, and third-to-last paragraph; I indicate the omissions here to avoid ellipses in the text.

'Of Kings' Treasuries', the 'Sesame' lecture from Ruskin's *Sesame and Lilies*, is included in this book not only to show Ruskin's ideas on reading, worthy in themselves and against which Proust defined his own, but also to show Proust's manner of reading (annotating, cross-referencing, arguing) in action. Ruskin's footnotes are noted as such; all the other notes are Proust's. About twenty per cent of 'Of Kings' Treasuries' had to be cut for space, so I took out what one might call 'political' material, although Ruskin would be the first to deny the distinction between matters of reading and matters of ethical action – as *Sesame and Lilies* makes clear, Ruskin shared the theory of language best described by Thoreau in his Journal in praise of John Brown: 'the one great rule of composition – and if I were a professor of rhetoric I should insist on this – is to *speak the truth*. This first, this second, this third.'

The Proustian and Ruskinian universes are vast and full of echoes, and tempting though it was for me to add my own connections and remembrances, offer my own makeshift memory, I have refrained from adding further translator's notes, explanatory or cross-referential. The layers of reading and reinterpretation already present in this book – Ruskin's writing, Proust's translation, Proust's notes, my own translation and selection and introduction, Eric Karpeles' foreword – make yet another layer prohibitive, and since many of Proust's notes had to be omitted for space, it seemed wrong to add notes of mine. Besides, as Borges says, 'I was a hospitable reader in those days, and I accepted everything with providential and enthusiastic resignation; I believed everything, even errata and poor illustrations.' Thus I neither correct nor indicate the omissions in Proust's inexact quotations (you can see his method by comparing §6 of 'Of Kings' Treasuries' with his quotation of that passage in 'On Reading', pp. 19–20). When giving the passages Proust quotes, I skip words and phrases to reflect as faithfully as possible Proust's condensations; I also use original English texts throughout rather than retranslating Proust's French, foregoing the cheap pleasure of translation gotchas as well as the more interesting matter of Proust's sometimes substantive and arguably intentional mistranslations. 'Of Kings' Treasuries' in particular is Ruskin's original, with my omissions (which are not Proust's) indicated by bracketed ellipses.

Most of the Proust material in this book has been translated into English before, although his notes and prefaces have never appeared together with Ruskin's full (or almost full) texts. I referred to, and learned much from, Jean Autret and William Burford's translation *On Reading* (1971), reprinted in *On Reading Ruskin: Prefaces to* La Bible d'Amiens *and* Sésame et les Lys *with Selections from the Notes to the Translated Texts* (1987); the other translations in the latter volume, namely Jean Autret and Phillip J. Wolfe's of the preface to *La Bible d'Amiens* and William Burford's of selected notes to *Sésame et les Lys*; John Sturrock's translations in *Against Sainte-Beuve and Other Essays* (1988), reprinted in *Days of Reading* (2008); and Euan Cameron's translations of relevant passages in Jean-Yves Tadié's *Marcel Proust: A Life* (2000). My source texts were the Library Edition of Ruskin's works, Antoine Compagnon's edition of *Sésame et les Lys, précédé de Sur la lecture* (1987), and Yves Michel-Ergal's of *La Bible d'Amiens* (2007); I also referred to the earlier editions of the French volumes available online. For information about Proust, I relied on Tadié's biography and the notes by Pierre Clarac and Yves Sandre in the 1971 Pléiade edition of *Contre Sainte-Beuve, précédé de Pastiches et mélanges et suivi de Essais et articles*. I would also like to acknowledge Sylvia Townsend Warner's 1958 translation *Marcel Proust On Art and Literature: 1896–1919*, where I first read Proust's essays, and the classic three-volume black-and-silver C.K. Scott Moncrieff and Terence Kilmartin translation of *Remembrance of Things Past*.

On Reading

On Reading
Translator's Preface to *Sesame and Lilies*[1]

To Princess Alexandre de Caraman-Chimay, whose Notes on Florence would have delighted Ruskin, I respectfully dedicate, as a token of my deep admiration for her, these pages that I have gathered together because they pleased her. M.P.

This translation into English is dedicated to Danielle, as a souvenir of our own travels, fondly remembered, among the canals and convents of Holland, the Hôtel-Dieu in Beaune, and family meals in central France. D.S.

There are perhaps no days of our childhood that we lived as fully as the days we think we left behind without living at all: the days we spent with a favourite book. Everything that filled others'

---

1. In this preface I want only to reflect in my own way on the subject that Ruskin treats in 'Of Kings' Treasuries': the uses of Reading. These pages, where there is hardly any mention of Ruskin, also constitute, if you will, a sort of criticism of his position. By laying out my own ideas, I find myself involuntarily and pre-emptively setting them up against his. In terms of direct commentary, the notes I have placed at the bottom of almost every page of Ruskin's text are enough. So I would have nothing further to add here, were I not anxious to reiterate my acknowledgment of my friend Marie Nordlinger, who, with far better things to do – her beautiful work as a sculptor, in which she shows such great originality and mastery – was still willing to revise this translation in detail, often making it far less imperfect. I would also like to thank, for all the valuable information he was willing to give me, the poet and scholar Charles Newton Scott, to whom we owe *The Church and Kindness to Animals* and *The Age of Marie Antoinette*, two fascinating books full of knowledge, sensitivity, and spirit that deserve to be far better known in France.

P.S.– This translation was already at the printer's when the volume containing *Sesame and Lilies* in the magnificent Library Edition of Ruskin's works, published by George Allen and edited by E.T. Cook and Alexander

days, so it seems, but that we avoided as vulgar impediments to a sacred pleasure – the game for whose sake a friend came looking for us right at the most interesting paragraph; the bothersome bee or sunbeam that forced us to look up from the book, or change position; the treats we had been forced to bring along but that we left untouched on the bench next to us while above our head the sun grew weaker in the blue sky; the dinner we had to go home for, during which we had no thought except to escape upstairs and finish, as soon as we were done, the interrupted chapter – our reading should have kept us from perceiving all that as anything other than obtrusive demands, but on the contrary, it has graven into us such happy memories of these things (memories much more valuable to us now than what we were reading with such passion at the time) that if, today, we happen to leaf through the pages of these books of the past, it is only because they are the sole calendars we have left of those bygone days, and we turn their pages in the hope of seeing reflected there the houses and lakes which are no more.

Wedderburn, appeared (July, 1905). I hastened to recall my manuscript, hoping to supplement certain of my notes with the help of Cook and Wedderburn's. Unfortunately, though their edition was of immeasurable interest to me, it was not able to help me with my book as much as I would have liked. Most of the references were, of course, already given in my own notes. The Library Edition did, however, supply some new information. I appended the words 'the Library Edition informs us' in such places, for I never took any information without immediately noting down where I was taking it from. As for the connections to the rest of Ruskin's works, it will be seen that the Library Edition refers to some works which I do not bring up, and that I refer to some other works unmentioned there. Readers unacquainted with my preface to the translation of *The Bible of Amiens* may perhaps feel that here, as a second commentator, I should have made more use of Cook and Wedderburn's references. Other readers, who understand what I intend with these translations, will not be surprised to learn that I have not done so. These connections to Ruskin's other works, as I see them, are essentially individual. They are a flash of memory and nothing more, a glimmer of one sensibility suddenly sparking between two different passages. And the light they cast is not as accidental as it seems. To supplement them

Who does not remember, as I do, this vacation-time reading that you tried to tuck away into one hour of the day after another, into every moment peaceful and inviolable enough to give it refuge. In the morning, after coming back from the park, when everyone had left 'to go for a stroll', I would slip into the dining room where, until lunch, still such a long time away, no one would come in except for old Félicie, who was relatively quiet, and where my only companions, very considerate of my reading, were the painted plates hung with hooks on the wall, the calendar whose previous day's page had just been torn off, and the grandfather clock and the fire, both of which talked without asking you to answer them, and whose gentle speech, empty of meaning, never replaced, as people's words do, the meaning of the word you were reading. I settled into a chair near the little wood fire, about which my uncle, a gardener and an early riser, would say: 'No harm in that! We can certainly stand a little fire in the fireplace; it was pretty cold in the kitchen garden at six o'clock, let me tell you. And to think, only

with additional, artificially contrived connections that have not flashed forth from my own depths would be to falsify the view of Ruskin I am using them to try to give. The Library Edition also supplies a vast amount of historical or biographical information, often of great interest. It will be seen that I have noted this information when I could, but on the whole seldom. First, this information did not absolutely answer the purpose which I had set for myself. Second, the Library Edition, as a purely scholarly edition, does not provide any commentary on Ruskin's text; it thus has more room for all the new documents and previously unpublished works whose publication is, in truth, the real purpose of the edition. I, on the other hand, accompany Ruskin's text with a constant stream of commentary, giving this unfortunately overburdened volume too large a size to permit the addition of unpublished documents, variants, and so forth. (I have had to forego including Ruskin's Prefaces, as well as the third lecture which Ruskin later added to the two original lectures of *Sesame and Lilies*.) All of this is said to excuse myself for not having made further use of Cook and Wedderburn's notes, and also to express my admiration for their truly definitive edition of Ruskin, one which is of very great interest to all of his readers.

a week until Easter!' Before lunch, which would, alas, put an end to my reading, still lay two long hours. From time to time you could hear the sound of the pump when the water was about to come out, which made you look up and out at it through the closed window, there, right nearby, on the only path in the garden, one which gave the beds of pansies a border of bricks and half-moons of pottery: pansies gathered, it seemed, from skies too beautiful to hold them, skies variegated as if reflecting back the windows of the church you could sometimes see between the roofs of the village, sad skies that appeared before a storm, or afterwards, too late, when the day was almost done. Unfortunately, the cook would come in long before lunch, to set the table; if only she could do it without talking! But she felt obliged to say, 'You must not be comfortable like that, should I move the table a little closer?' And merely in order to answer 'No, thank you' it was necessary to come to a dead stop and bring back your voice from afar, the voice within your lips that had been swiftly and silently repeating all the words your eyes were reading; you had to bring that voice to a stop, send it out of your mouth, and, to manage a respectable 'No, thank you', give it a semblance of ordinary life again, the tone of communication and interaction it had lost. The hour went by. People often began to arrive in the dining room long before lunch, either the ones who had gotten tired and cut short their walk, had 'taken the Méséglise way,' or the ones who had not gone out at all that morning, because they 'had some writing to do'. They would say the requisite 'I don't want to disturb you' but immediately start to go up to the fire, look at the clock, announce that they wouldn't be sorry to see lunchtime arrive. The one who had 'stayed home to write' would be met with a peculiar deference, and people would say 'So, you've attended to your little "correspondence"?' with a smile in which there was respect, mystery, indulgence, and consideration, as though this 'little correspondence' were at one and the same time a state secret, a royal prerogative, a stroke of luck, and a touch of illness. Some people, without waiting any longer, sat down early in their place at the table – a devastating development, because it set a bad example for the others coming in, made them think it was already noon, and led my parents to say all too soon the fatal words: 'Come on, shut your book, it's time for lunch.' Everything was ready, the table was set with everything on the tablecloth except the items that were not brought out until the end of the meal: the glass apparatus in which my uncle, the horticulturist and cook, made the coffee himself at the table; the device had complicated tubes like some scientific instrument, it smelled good, and it was fun to see the sudden burst of boiling bubbles ascend into the glass globe and leave a fragrant brown ash on its clouded surface; then, too, the strawberries and cream which this same uncle mixed together, always in exactly the same proportions, stopping at precisely the requisite pink, with the experience of an expert colorist and the foresight of a gourmand. How long lunch seemed to me! My great-aunt only tasted each dish to give her opinion about it, mildly enough so that opposing judgments could be suggested, if never actually accepted. She was an excellent judge of novels and poems, but on such topics she always relied, with a feminine humility, on the opinions of more competent authorities. There, in such wavering realms of caprice, she thought, a single individual's taste was in no position to ascertain the truth. But when it came to the things whose rules and principles her mother had taught her – how certain dishes should be prepared, how Beethoven's sonatas should be played, how a guest should be made to feel welcome – she knew she possessed the correct idea of perfection and could discern the greater or lesser extent to which others approached it. Besides, perfection in these three matters meant almost the same thing: a sort of simplicity of means, sobriety, and charm. She recoiled with horror from adding spices to a dish that did not absolutely require them, abusing the pedals by playing with affectation, or, while 'receiving', speaking too much about oneself or any departure from perfect naturalness. From the first bite, the first notes, an ordinary invitation, she claimed to know whether she was dealing with a good cook, a true musician, a well brought up woman. 'She may have a lot more fingers to work with than I do, but she's lacking in taste, to play that simple andante with so much emphasis.' 'She may be a very brilliant woman, full of good qualities, but it's tactless to talk about herself that way.' 'She may well be a very knowledgeable cook, but she doesn't know how make steak and potatoes.' Steak and potatoes! The ideal competition piece, difficult precisely in its simplicity, a sort of *Sonate Pathétique* of cooking, the gastronomical equivalent of, in social life, the visit of a lady who comes to ask you for information about a maid, and who, in this simple act, can show the extent of her tact and education or lack thereof. My grandfather was proud enough to want every dish to have been a success, but was too poor a judge of cooking to know when it had failed. He was willing to sometimes admit that it had, but he did so very rarely, and always as though it had happened purely by chance. My great-aunt's always justified criticism, on the other hand, which implied that the cook had actually not known how to make the dish, could not help but be particularly intolerable to my grandfather. Often, to avoid an argument with him, my great-aunt, after a tiny nibble, did not give her opinion, from which we knew immediately that it was not favorable. She kept quiet but we read a considered and unshakeable disapproval in her gentle eyes, which had the power to make my grandfather furious. He begged her, his voice thick with irony, to favour us with her opinion, grew impatient with her silence, plied her with questions, lost his temper, but you could tell that she would be led to the stake rather than confess what my grandfather believed, that the cream in the dessert was not too sweet.

After lunch I took up my reading again at once; especially if the day was a bit hot, everyone went upstairs 'to retire' to their rooms, which allowed me to return to mine right away, up the little staircase of close-set stairs. The room was on the only upper floor, but low enough that a child could jump down from the projecting windows and find himself on the street. I would go to close my window, unable to avoid the greetings of the gunsmith across the street who, under the pretext of lowering the awning, came out every day after lunch to smoke a cigarette in front of his door and say hello to the passers-by who sometimes stopped to chat. The theories of William Morris, so assiduously put into practice by Maple and the English decorators, dictate that a room is beautiful only on the condition that it contain only things that are useful to us, and furthermore that every one of these useful things, even an ordinary nail, be apparent, not concealed. Reproductions of a few masterpieces are permitted on the naked walls of these sanitary chambers, above the brass and completely uncovered bed. Judged by these aesthetic principles, my room was not beautiful in the least, because it was full of things which could serve no purpose at all and which modestly concealed whatever objects did serve a purpose, to the point of making them extremely hard to use. But it was precisely those useless things, there not for my convenience but rather seemingly for their own pleasure, which gave the room beauty in my eyes. Those high white curtains concealing from view the bed that was set back as though nestled in a shrine; the marceline comforters, floral bedspreads, embroidered coverlets, and batiste pillowcases strewn across the bed, under which it disappeared during the day, like an altar in the Month of the Virgin Mary under festoons and flowers, and which, in the evening, so that I could go to sleep, I would carefully put on an armchair where they agreed to spend the night; next to the bed, the trinity of a glass with blue designs on it, a matching sugar bowl, and the carafe (always empty, since the day after my arrival, on the orders of my aunt, who was afraid of seeing me 'spill'), like instruments of worship – almost as sacred as the precious orange-flower liqueur placed near them in a glass vial – which I would have no more thought of

9

profaning, or even thought myself able to use for my own personal needs, than if they had been consecrated pyxes, but which I contemplated at great length before getting undressed, afraid to knock them over with a clumsy movement; the little crocheted stoles which threw over the backs of the armchairs a cloak of white roses that must not have lacked thorns too, because every time I had finished reading and wanted to get up I discovered that I was caught fast on their little hooks; the glass bell under which, isolated from vulgar touch, the clock gossiped in private to seashells brought from far away and an old sentimental flower, but which was so heavy that when the clock stopped no one but the clockmaker would have been foolhardy enough to try to wind it up again; the white guipure-lace cloth which, thrown like an altar-cloth over a chest of drawers adorned with two vases, a picture of the Savior, and a blessed palm, made that chest resemble a communion table (and this image received the finishing touch from a prie-dieu, tucked away there every day after the room had been 'done'), but whose frayed edges were always getting caught in the cracks of the drawers and bringing their movement to a complete halt, so that I could never so much as get a handkerchief out without making the picture of the Savior, the holy vases, and the blessed palm fall over, all at the same time, and without stumbling and clutching the prie-dieu to steady myself; finally, the triple layers of light gauze curtains, heavy toile curtains, and heavier damask curtains, always smiling on me in their whiteness reminiscent of hawthorn, often glowing in the sunlight, but ultimately very annoying in their awkward, stubborn insistence on playing around the parallel wooden curtain rods and getting tangled up with each other and caught in the window whenever I wanted to open or close it, a second one always ready, whenever I man-aged to free the first, to take its place in the joints as perfectly designed to snatch it up as a real hawthorn bush would have been, or the nests of swallows who had taken it into their heads to settle there, so that the act of opening or closing my casement window, apparently so simple, was one I was never able to manage without the help of someone else from the house; – all these things, which not only were unable to answer a single one of my needs but produced obstacles (even if minor) to the satisfaction of those needs, and which obviously had never been put there for anyone's use, filled the room with in some sense personal thoughts, with an atmosphere of idiosyncratic preference, as though they themselves had chosen to live there and it pleased them: the same feeling that trees give off in a clearing, or flowers along paths and by old stone walls. These objects filled the room with a silent and multifarious life, with a mystery in which my own personality found itself at once lost and enchanted; they turned the room into a kind of chapel where the sun, when it passed through the little red windowpanes that my uncle had intercalated at the top of the window, pricked at the walls after turning the hawthorns of the curtains pink, its rays as alien and disconcerting as if the little chapel had been ringed by a surrounding nave of stained glass windows, and where the sound of the bells arrived so resoundingly, due to the proximity of our house to the church – in addition, the temporary altars during the major holidays connected us to the church with a path of flowers – that I could imagine them ringing inside our roof, just above the window from which I often greeted the priest with his breviary, my aunt coming home from vespers, or the altar-boy bringing us some consecrated bread. As for Brown's photograph of Botticelli's *Spring* or the plaster cast of *The Unknown Woman* from the Lille Museum on the walls and the mantelpiece in Maple's rooms – William Morris's only concessions to useless beauty – I must confess that my room had instead a kind of engraving that depicted Prince Eugene, terrifying and handsome in his hussar jacket, and whom I was quite astonished to see one night in a great din of locomotives and hail, still terrifying and handsome, by the door to a restaurant in a train station, serving as an advertisement for a brand of biscuits.

I now suspect that my grandfather had once been given the engraving as a gift from a generous manufacturer, before putting it up in my room forever. But back then I didn't care where it had come from; its origins seemed to me historical and mysterious, and I didn't imagine that there could be multiple copies of the being I saw as a real person, a permanent resident of the room that I only shared with him, where I rediscovered him every year, always the same. It is a very long time now since I have seen him and I suppose I shall never see him again. But if such good fortune ever should come to pass, I think he would have far more to tell me than Botticelli's *Spring*. I will leave it to men and women of taste to decorate their homes with reproductions of the masterpieces they admire, unburdening their memory of the task of preserving a truly valuable image of those masterpieces by entrusting it to a carved wooden frame. I will leave it to men and women of taste to turn their room into the very picture of that taste, and to fill it solely with objects their taste can approve of. As for me, I feel myself live and think only in rooms where everything is the creation, the language, of lives profoundly different from my own, of a taste opposed to mine, where I can find nothing of my own conscious thoughts, where my imagination is excited by feeling itself driven into the heart of the not-me; I feel happy only when I set foot in one of those provincial hotels – on Avenue de la Gare, on the church square, by the harbour – with long, cold hallways where the wind from outside battles and defeats the best efforts of the radiator, where the detailed map of the neighbourhood is yet again the only décor on the walls, where every sound serves only to make the silence appear by shifting it somewhere else, where the rooms have a musty smell that the strong draught scrubs but does not remove and that the nostrils inhale a hundred times in order to carry it to the imagination, which is enchanted with it, which makes it pose like a model so that it can try to re-create it inside itself with all the thoughts and memories it contains;

where, in the evening, when you open the door to your room, you have the feeling of breaking in on the life that lies scattered there, of taking it boldly in hand when, the door having closed again, you enter deeply into the room and walk up to the table or the window; the feeling of sitting down with that life in a sort of easy promiscuity on the sofa that an upholsterer in this provincial capital has done up in what he imagined to be the Parisian style; the feeling of caressing every inch of that life's naked flesh, in the hope of arousing yourself with the liberties you are taking, when you put your things here and there, play the master in this room that is filled to overflowing with others' souls and that preserves the imprint of their dreams even in the shape of the andirons and the design of the curtains, when you walk barefoot on its unknown carpet – it is a hidden life you have the feeling of locking up with you when you go, trembling all over, to bolt the door, of pushing in front of you onto the bed, and finally of lying with under large white sheets which come up over your face while nearby the bells of the church toll for the whole city the insomniac hours of dying men and lovers.

I had not been reading in my room a very long time when I had to go out to the park, about half a mile from the village.[2] But after the game I was forced to play, I would cut short my tasting of the treats that had been carried out in baskets and handed out to the children alongside the river, on the grass where the book had been put down with orders not to pick it up again. A little farther on, in certain of the park's rather wild and mysterious depths, the river ceased to be a rectilinear and artificial body of water bedecked with swans and bordered by paths where statues stood smiling, and instead rushed onward, now jumping with carp, at high speed past the park fence and turned into a river in the geographical sense of the word –

2. What we called, for some reason, a village is actually the main city of the region, with almost 3,000 inhabitants, according to the Guide Joanne.

a river deserving a name – before quickly flowing out (was it really the same water as the water between the statues, beneath the swans?) into the pastures where cattle lay sleeping, where it inundated the golden buttercups: a kind of meadow which the river turned marshy and which was joined to the village on one side by the crude towers that were left over, it was said, from the Middle Ages, and was joined to 'nature' on the other side by means of the ascending paths of wild rose and hawthorn trees – a 'nature' extending to infinity, to villages bearing other names, to the unknown. I would let the others finish eating down in the park, by the swans, and run up into the maze, to a bower where I could sit and not be found, with my back to the clipped hazelnut tree, and from there I could see the asparagus plants, the fringes of strawberry bushes, the pond into which, on some days, horses hitched to a wheel would pump water, the white gate up higher that was 'the end of the park', and beyond it the fields of cornflower and poppy. In this bower the silence was deep and the risk of being discovered almost nonexistent, a safety rendered even sweeter by the distant cries down below, calling me in vain, sometimes even approaching, climbing the lower slopes, searching everywhere, before going back down, not having found what they were looking for; then no other sound; only, from time to time, the golden sound of the bells that, far away across the pastures, seemed to toll behind the blue sky and might have warned me of the passing hours, but I, surprised by how soft they sounded and disturbed by the deeper silence that followed after their last chimes had been emptied out of it, was never sure what time it had tolled. These were not the thundering bells that you heard when you returned to the village – when you neared the church that, from close up, regained its great, rigid height, its slate-gray cowl dotted with black crows rearing up into the evening blue – letting fly their bursts of sound across the square 'for the bounties of the earth'. These bells reached the park only weakly, softly, and addressed themselves not to me but to the whole countryside, all the villages, all the lonely farmers in their fields; they in no way compelled me to raise my head, they passed close by me, bearing the time of day into the distant countryside, without noticing me, without recognising me, and without disturbing me.

And sometimes, at home, in my bed, long after dinner, the last hours of the evening also sheltered my reading, but only on the days when I had reached the final chapters of a book, when there was not much more to read to get to the end. Then, risking both punishment if I was discovered and the insomnia that, once I had finished the book, might last all night, I re-lit my candle after my parents went to bed; in the street outside, between the gunsmith's house and the post office, bathed in silence, the sky was dark but nonetheless blue and full of stars, and to the left, on the raised lane just at the turn where its elevated ascent began, you could feel watching you the monstrous black apse of the church whose sculptures did not sleep at night – just a village church but still of historical importance, the magical abode of the Lord, of the consecrated bread, of multicoloured saints, and of the ladies from the neighboring chateaux who, on feast days, making the hens squawk and the gossips stare, crossed the marketplace in their 'turn-out' to go to mass and, on their way back, after leaving the shadow of the porch where the faithful, pushing open the vestibule door, scattered the errant rubies of the nave, did not pass the pastry shop on the square without buying one of those cakes in the shape of a tower, protected from the sun by an awning – 'manqués', 'Saint-Honorés', 'Genoese' – cakes whose leisurely, sugary scent remains mixed in my mind with the bells of high mass and the happiness of Sundays.

When the last page had been read, the book was finished. With a deep sigh I had to halt the frantic racing of my eyes and of my voice, which had followed after my eyes without making a sound, stopping only to catch its breath. Then, to give the turmoil within me (unleashed too long to be able to calm down on its own) other movements to occupy itself with, I would stand up and walk back and forth next to my bed, my eyes still fixed on a point which one would have sought in vain within the room, or outside the room either, for it was located at a distance of the soul and nowhere else – one of those distances that cannot be measured in feet or miles like other distances, and that moreover it is impossible to confuse with the other kind of distance when you look at the 'faraway' eyes of someone whose thoughts are 'elsewhere'. And now what? Is that all there was to the book? These beings to whom we had given more of our attention and affection than we give to the people in our life, not always daring to admit the extent to which we loved them, so that we even feigned boredom or closed the book with pretended indifference when our parents came upon us while we were reading and seemed to smile at our emotion; these people for whom we had panted and sobbed – we would never see them again, never learn anything more about them. Already, for a few pages in a cruel 'Epilogue', the author had taken care to 'trail off', leaving more and more space between the characters with an indifference simply unbelievable to anyone who knew the interest with which he had followed them, step by step, until that point. What these people did with every hour of their lives was told to us and then, suddenly: 'Twenty years after these events, you might have

3. I confess that a certain way of using the imperfect indicative in French – that cruel tense which gives us life as something both ephemeral and passive, and which, at the very moment it retraces our actions, stamps them with illusion and annihilates them in a bygone past, without leaving us the consolation of activity as the perfect tense does – has remained for me an inexhaustible source of mysterious sadnesses. Even now, I may have thought about death calmly for hours, but if I merely open a volume of Sainte-Beuve's *Monday Conversations* and stumble upon, for instance, this sentence spoken by Lamartine about Madame d'Albany: 'Nothing about her at that time *recalled*..... She *was* a small woman whose figure, sinking slightly beneath her weight, had lost...' – I suddenly feel myself overwhelmed by the deepest melancholy. In novels, authors so obviously intend to make us suffer that we brace ourselves for it a little more.

met an old man on the streets of Fougères, his back not yet bent by age...'3 Having spent two volumes letting us glimpse the delightful possibilities of a certain marriage, having frightened us and then delighted us with every obstacle encountered and then overcome, the author let us learn from a passing comment by a secondary character that the marriage had taken place, we don't know exactly when or how – this astonishing epilogue seemed to have been written from the heights of heaven by someone who cared nothing for our transient passions, someone substituted somehow for our author. How we wanted the book to keep going, and, if that were not possible, wanted more information about all of its characters, wanted to learn something further about their lives, and spend our own on matters not altogether foreign to the love that they inspired within us,4 whose object we had suddenly lost; how we wanted not to have loved in vain, for an hour, those beings who tomorrow will be nothing but names on a forgotten page, in a book that has nothing to do with life, and whose value we had seriously mistaken, since its fate here below, we now understand (and our parents inform us, if necessary, with a contemptuous word), was

4. We can attempt this, in a sort of roundabout way, in the case of books that have a historical basis and are not wholly fictional. Balzac, for example, whose works are in a sense impure mixtures of the spirit and an insufficiently transformed reality, lends himself singularly well to this kind of reading. Or at least he has found the best of these 'historical readers' in Albert Sorel, who has written incomparable essays about *The Gondreville Mystery* and *The Wrong Side of Paris*. Reading itself, moreover – this pleasure at once ardent and level-headed – how well it seems to suit Sorel, with his seeker's spirit and calm and powerful body: reading, during which the thousand sensations of poetry and obscure well-being, soaring jubilantly up from a foundation of good health, create around the reader's reveries a pleasure as sweet and golden as honey.

It is not only in Sorel's studies of semi-historical works, moreover, that his way of including so much original and strong reflection in an act of reading has been brought to perfection. I will always remember, with profound gratitude, that my translation of *The Bible of Amiens* was the subject of perhaps the most powerful pages he has ever written.

not in the least to contain the whole of the world and all of destiny, as we had thought, but simply to occupy a very narrow place on a notary's bookshelf, between the undistinguished annals of the *Illustrated Magazine of Fashion* and the *Geography of the Eure-et-Loir Region*...

* * *

Before attempting to show, at the threshold of 'Of Kings' Treasuries', why Reading cannot in my opinion play the dominating role in life that Ruskin assigns to it in this little work of his, I have felt obliged to make an exception for that enchanting childhood reading whose memory must remain sacred to us all. Doubtless I have shown only too well, by the length and the character of the preceding pages, what I asserted at the start: that what our childhood reading leaves behind in us is above all the image of the places and days where and when we engaged in it. I have not escaped its sorcery: intending to speak about reading I have spoken of everything but books, because it is not of books that the reading itself has spoken to me. But maybe the memories it has given back to me, one after the other, will themselves have awakened in the reader – will have gradually led the reader, with all these delays on flowered and winding paths, to recreate in his own mind – the original psychological act called *Reading*, and done so with enough force to enable him now to follow, as though within himself, the various reflections which remain for me to present here.

'Of Kings' Treasuries' is a lecture on reading that Ruskin delivered at the Rusholme Town Hall, Manchester, on 6 December 1864, to benefit a library fund at the Rusholme Institute. On December 14, he delivered a second lecture, 'Of Queens' Gardens', on the role of women, to benefit the establishment of a school in Ancoats. 'All through that year, 1864,' W.G. Collingwood writes in his excellent *The Life and Work of Ruskin*, 'he remained at home, except for frequent evenings with Carlyle. And when, in December, he gave those lectures at Manchester which afterwards, as *Sesame and Lilies*, became his most popular work,[5] we can trace his better health of mind and body in the brighter tone of his thought. We can hear the echo of Carlyle's talk in the heroic, aristocratic, Stoic ideals, and in the insistence on the value of books and free public libraries,– Carlyle being the founder of the London Library...'

Since I want here only to discuss Ruskin's thesis in itself, without regard to its historical origins, we might sum it up rather exactly with these words of Descartes: 'The reading of all good books is indeed like a conversation with the most upstanding persons of past centuries – their authors.' Ruskin may not have known this somewhat arid reflection by the French philosopher, but in fact it can be found everywhere in Ruskin's lecture, only it has been wrapped in an Apollonian gold with the English fogs melted into it, like the gold whose glory illuminates the landscapes of his favorite painter, Turner. 'Granting,' he writes, 'that we had both the will and the sense to choose our friends well, how few of us have the power, how limited is the sphere of choice. We cannot know whom we would... We may, by good fortune, obtain a glimpse of a great poet, and hear the sound of his voice; or put a question to a man of science, and be answered good-humouredly. We may intrude ten minutes' talk on a cabinet minister, or have, once in our lives, the privilege of arresting the glance of a queen.

5. This book was later enlarged by the addition of a third lecture, 'The Mystery of Life and Its Arts', to the original two. Popular editions still contain only 'Of Kings' Treasuries' and 'Of Queens' Gardens'. The present volume translates only these first two lectures, and also omits the several prefaces Ruskin wrote for various editions of *Sesame and Lilies*. The scope of this volume and the abundance of my own commentary permit nothing more. Except for four editions (Smith, Elder, and Co.), the many editions of *Sesame and Lilies* have all been published by George Allen, the renowned publisher of all of Ruskin's work and the head of Ruskin House.

And yet these momentary chances we covet; and spend our years, and passions, and powers, in pursuit of little more than these; while, meantime, there is a society continually open to us, of people who will talk to us as long as we like, whatever our rank. And this society, because it is so numerous and so gentle, and can be kept waiting round us all day long,– kings and statesmen lingering patiently, not to grant audience, but to gain it! – we never go to seek it out, in those plainly furnished ante-rooms, our bookcase shelves,– never listen to a word they would say!'[6] 'You may tell me, perhaps,' Ruskin adds, 'that if you prefer the company of living men, it is because you can see their faces', but he refutes that first objection and then a second; he shows that reading is precisely a conversation with men much wiser and more interesting than those we can know in person. I have tried to show, in the notes with which I have accompanied my translation, that reading cannot be equated like this to conversation, even a conversation with the wisest of men; that the essential difference between a book and a friend is not their greater or lesser wisdom but the manner in which we communicate with them – reading, unlike conversation, consists for each of us in receiving the communication of another thought while remaining alone, or in other words, while continuing to bring into play the mental powers we have in solitude and which conversation immediately puts to flight; while remaining open to inspiration, the soul still hard at its fruitful labours upon itself. If Ruskin had drawn the proper inferences from the other truths he states a few pages later, he would probably have come to a conclusion analogous to my own. But clearly he was not trying to get to the heart of the idea of reading. To instruct us in the value of reading, he wanted merely to recount for us a kind of beautiful Platonic myth, with the simplicity of the Greeks who have revealed to us almost all

6. *Sesame and Lilies*, 'Of Kings' Treasuries', §6.

the true ideas and left to scrupulous modernity the task of thoroughly plumbing their depths. But even if I think that reading, in its essence, this fruitful miracle of communication in the bosom of solitude, is something more, something other that what Ruskin says it is, I nevertheless do not think that we can grant it the preponderant role in our spiritual life which Ruskin seems to assign to it.

The limits to the role of reading derive from the nature of its virtues. And it is once again childhood reading that I will turn to in order to investigate what these virtues consist of. The book you have seen me reading just now by the fireplace in the dining room, in my bedroom deep in the armchair with its crocheted head-rest, and during the beautiful afternoon hours under the hazelnut trees and the hawthorns of the park, where every breeze from the immeasurable fields came from so far away to play silently around me, offering up to my inattentive nostrils, without a word, the scent of the clover and sainfoin to which I would sometimes raise my tired eyes – since your eyes, straining toward that book at a distance of twenty years, may not be able to make out its title, my memory, whose vision is better suited to this type of perception, will tell you what it was: *Captain Fracasse* by Théophile Gautier. Above all, I loved in it two or three sentences which seemed to me the most original and beautiful in the book. I could not imagine that any other author could ever have written anything comparable. But I had the feeling that their beauty corresponded to a reality that Gautier let us glimpse only a little corner of, once or twice per volume. And since I thought that he surely must know it in its entirety, I wanted to read other books of his in which all the sentences would be as beautiful as these, and would be about things I wanted to know his opinions on. 'Laughter is not at all cruel by nature; it distinguishes man from beast, and it is, as stands written in the *Odyssey* of the Grecian Poet Homerus, the privilege of the blessed, immortal deities who laugh Olympian peals to while away all the hours of eternity.'[7] This sentence brought me to a state of true intoxication. I thought I could perceive a marvelous antiquity through those Middle Ages that only Gautier could reveal to me. But I would have preferred it if, instead of saying it surreptitiously, after a long, boring description of a castle with so many words I didn't know the meaning of that I couldn't imagine it at all, he had written a book of nothing but sentences like this, and had spoken of things that, after his book was finished, I could continue to know and love. I would have preferred it if he, the one wise custodian of truth, had told me the correct opinion I should have of Shakespeare, of Saintine, of Sophocles, Euripides, Silvio Pellico whom I had read during an unusually cold March, pacing back and forth, stamping my feet, and running along the paths every time I shut the book in the exaltation of having just finished reading, of the energy stored up during my immobility, and of the bracing wind blowing down the village streets. Above all, I would have wanted him to tell me if I had a better or worse chance of arriving at the truth if I repeated my sixth grade class, or if I became a diplomat when I grew up, or a lawyer at the

7. In truth, this sentence will not be found in *Captain Fracasse*, at least not in this form. Instead of 'as stands written in the *Odyssey* of the Grecian Poet,' the text has simply 'as Homerus says'. But since the expressions 'as stands written in Homerus' and 'as stands written in the *Odyssey*', which do appear elsewhere in the book, gave me the same quality of pleasure, I have permitted myself to fuse these several beauties together into one to make the example more striking for the reader, especially since, truth to tell, I no longer have for them the same pious reverence. In still other places in *Captain Fracasse*, Homer is described as 'the Grecian Poet', and I am sure that that enchanted me as well. In any case, I can no longer recapture these forgotten pleasures precisely enough to be sure that I have not overstepped the mark, have not gone too far in piling all of these marvels into a single sentence. I don't believe that I have, though. And it pains me to think that my ecstatic recital of a sentence from *Captain Fracasse* to the irises and periwinkles bent over the riverbanks with the path's pebbles under my feet would have been even more pleasurable if I had been able to find in a single sentence of Gautier's all the charms I have artificially brought together today without, alas, it giving me any pleasure at all.

appellate courts. But as soon as the beautiful sentence was finished, he started describing a table covered 'with a layer of dust so thick that you could trace words in it with your finger', something so insignificant in my eyes that I could not pay it the slightest attention; and I was reduced to wondering what other books Gautier had written that might better satisfy my longing and finally let me know the entirety of his thought.

Indeed, this is one of the great and wondrous characteristics of beautiful books (and one which enables us to understand the simultaneously essential and limited role that reading can play in our spiritual life): that for the author they may be called *Conclusions*, but for the reader, *Provocations*. We can feel that our wisdom begins where the author's ends, and we want him to give us answers when all he can do is give us desires. He awakens these desires in us only when he gets us to contemplate the supreme beauty which he cannot reach except through the utmost efforts of his art. But by a strange and, it must be said, providential law of spiritual optics (a law which signifies, perhaps, that we cannot receive the truth from anyone else, that we must create it ourselves), the end of a book's wisdom appears to us as merely the start of our own, so that at the moment when the book has told us everything it can, it gives rise to the feeling that it has told us nothing. Moreover, when we ask it questions it cannot answer, we are also asking for answers that would not tell us anything, because one effect of the love which poets awaken in us is to make us attach a literal importance to the things which for them are meaningful due to merely personal emotions. In every picture they paint for us, they seem to give us but a fleeting glimpse of a marvellous place unlike anywhere else in the world, and we want them to make us penetrate its heart. 'Bring us with you,' we wish we could say to Maeterlinck, to Madame de Noailles, into 'the Dutch garden where flowers long out of fashion grow', along the way perfumed 'with clover and artemisia', and to all the places on earth which you never told us about in your books but which you judge to be just as beautiful. We want to go see the field which

Millet shows us in his *Spring* (for painters instruct us the same way poets do), we want Claude Monet to lead us to Giverny, on the Seine, to the bend in the river that he barely lets us make out through the morning mist. Now in actual fact, it was purely the chance of friends or relations happening to invite them to pass through here or visit there that made Madame de Noailles, Maeterlinck, Millet, Claude Monet choose this road, this garden, this field, this bend in the river to depict rather than any other. What makes these places seem different to us, and more beautiful than anywhere else in the world, is that they bear, on their surface, like an elusive reflection, the impression they made on a genius, a reflection we would have seen playing, strangely and tyrannically, upon the indifferent and submissive surface of any other terrain that he or she depicted. This semblance with which the places charm us and deceive us, beyond which we want so much to go, is the very essence of that which, lacking a third dimension so to speak – a mirage frozen on a canvas – constitutes a vision. This mist that our eager eyes want to pierce: that is the last word of the painter's art. And the supreme efforts of the writer, like those of the painter, culminate in raising, only part way, the veil of ugliness and meaninglessness which makes us incurious about the universe. Then he says to us: 'Look, look,

'Perfumed with clover and artemisia,
Clasping their lively, narrow streams: the
Land of the Aisne and of the Oise.

'Look at the Dutch house in Zeeland, pink and shiny like a seashell. Look! Learn to see!' And at that very moment, he disappears. Such is the value of reading and also what it lacks. To turn it into a discipline in its own right is to give too great a role to what is merely an initiation. Reading is at the threshold of our inner life; it can lead us into that life but cannot constitute it.

There are nevertheless certain circumstances, pathological circumstances one might say, of spiritual depression, in which reading can become a sort of curative discipline entrusted with the task of continually leading a lazy spirit, by means of repeated excitations, back to an inner life. Books then play for the person in these circumstances a role analogous to that played by psychotherapists for certain neurasthenics. It is well known that in certain diseases of the nervous system, even if none of the organs themselves are affected, the sufferer is swallowed up in a kind of inability to will, as if trapped in a kind of deep rut and unable to pull himself out of it alone, where he would eventually waste away entirely if a strong helping hand were not held out to him. His brain, his legs, his stomach, his lungs are unharmed. He has no real incapacity that prevents him from working, walking, eating, being out in the cold, but he finds it impossible to will the various acts he is otherwise perfectly able to perform, and this inertia of the will would inevitably lead to an organic decay that ended up becoming the equivalent of the sickness he did not have unless the impulse he cannot find in himself comes to him from without, from a doctor who wills for him until the day when his various organic wills have little by little been rehabilitated. Now there are certain spirits we can compare to these sufferers, spirits whom a kind of laziness or frivolousness prevents from descending on their own into the deeper regions of themselves where true mental life begins.[8] It is not that, once led there, they are unable to discover and exploit these true riches, but

8. I feel the germ of this in Louis-Marcelin de Fontanes, about whom Sainte-Beuve has said: 'The epicurean side is very strongly developed in him... without these rather materialist habits, Fontanes, with all his talent, would have produced much more... and more lasting works.' Note how the impotent man always claims to be anything but. Fontanes writes:

Je perds mon temps s'il faut les croire,
Eux seuls du siècle sont l'honneur

[If they are to be believed I am wasting my time;
Only they do honor to the age]

and insists that he works very hard indeed.

without such outside intervention they live on the surface, in a perpetual forgetting of themselves, a kind of passivity which makes them the plaything of every pleasure and reduces them to the stature of those who surround them, jostling them this way and that; like the gentleman who, having led the life of a highway brigand since childhood, no longer remembers the name he has long since ceased to bear, they will end by abolishing in themselves every feeling, every memory, of their inner nobility, unless an exterior impulse comes to forcibly reintroduce them into mental life, where they will suddenly recapture the power to think for themselves and to create. Clearly this impulse, which the lazy spirit cannot find in itself and which has to come from another, can be received only in the bosom of solitude, outside of which, as we have seen, precisely the creative activity that is to be resurrected in him cannot occur. Nothing can result from the pure solitude of the lazy spirit, because that spirit is unable to set its creative activity in motion by itself, but even the loftiest conversation or the most insistent advice would not help it in the slightest either, because it cannot directly produce original activity. What is needed, therefore, is an intervention that occurs deep within ourselves while coming from someone else, the impulse of another mind that we receive in the bosom of solitude. As we have seen, this is precisely the definition of reading and fits nothing but reading.

Coleridge's case is even more pathological. 'No man of his time, perhaps of any time,' according to Carpenter (as quoted by Ribot in his fine book *The Diseases of the Will*), 'combined better than Coleridge the reasoning power of the philosopher, the imagination of the poet, etc. Yet there is no one who, gifted with such remarkable talents, accomplished so little: the great defect in his character was the lack of the will to make use of his natural gifts. For all of the massive projects constantly floating through his mind, he never made a serious effort to execute even one. Thus, at the start of his career, he found a generous bookseller who promised him thirty guineas for the poems he had been reciting... He preferred to come begging every week, without supplying a single line of the poems he had only to write down in order to free himself.'

Thus the only discipline which can exert a beneficial influence on such minds is reading: Q.E.D., as the geometers say. But here too, reading is merely a kind of instigation, which can in no way substitute for our personal activity; reading is happy simply to give us back the use of this ability, the way the psychotherapist, in the nervous ailments to which we have just alluded, merely restores the sufferer's will to use his stomach, his legs, his brain, all of which have remained unharmed. Whether or not every spirit shares this laziness to a greater or lesser extent, this stagnation in the worst cases, and whether or not the exaltation which follows certain kinds of reading may, without being strictly necessary, have a certain propitious influence on one's own labours, we may cite more than one writer who liked to read a beautiful page before sitting down to work. Emerson rarely began to write without re-reading several pages of Plato; Dante is not the only poet whom Virgil has brought to the threshold of paradise.

Insofar as reading initiates us, insofar as her magic key opens the door deep inside us to the dwelling places we would not otherwise have known how to reach, its role in our life is a salutary one. On the other hand, reading becomes dangerous when, instead of awakening us to an individual inner life, it takes its place: when truth no longer seems to us an ideal we can realise only by the intimate progression of our thoughts and the efforts of our heart, but instead starts to seem like a material thing deposited in the pages of books, like honey made by others, which we can taste, passively, in a perfect repose of body and mind, merely by taking the trouble to reach out our hand to the library shelf. It even happens sometimes, in certain rather exceptional and anyway, as we shall see, less dangerous cases, that the truth, still understood as external, is far away, hidden somewhere difficult to reach: in some private document, or unpublished letter, or obscure memoir that might shed an unexpected light on certain personalities. What happiness, what rest for a spirit exhausted by the search for the truth in himself, to be able to tell himself that the truth may be found somewhere else, between the folio pages of a volume jealously preserved in a Dutch convent, and if it requires a certain effort to reach it then at least these efforts will be physical and material, and for the mind merely a kind of respite, full of charm. It will no doubt be necessary to take a long journey, travel by passenger barge across marshes swept by a wailing wind while the reeds on the riverbank bend and raise their heads one after another in an undulation without end; it will be necessary to stop in Dordrecht, whose ivy-covered church is reflected in the tracery of sleeping canals and in the whispering waters of the Meuse, gilt with gold, where gliding vessels in the evening disturb the reflected straight lines of red roofs and blue sky; and, finally, having reached the end of the journey, we will still not be sure of getting to the truth. We will need to put powerful influences into play, befriend the venerable archbishop of Utrecht with his handsome square face like an old Jansenist's, and the pious keeper of the Amersfoort archives. The conquest of the truth in a case like this is understood to be like the success of a sort of diplomatic mission, in which neither difficulties of the journey nor hazards of negotiation are lacking. But so what? All the members of the tiny old church of Utrecht, on whose good will it depends whether or not we will enter into possession of the truth, are charming people whose faces, straight out of the seventeenth century, are a change from what we are used to; it will be amusing to stay in touch with them, if only by letter. The esteem they will continue to send us indications of from time to time will elevate us in our own eyes and we will preserve their letters as a guarantee of something, and a curiosity. And one day we will not fail to dedicate one of our books to them, which is certainly the least we can do for the people who have given us... the truth. As for the few inquiries, the brief labours we will be obliged to undertake in the convent library, indispensable preliminaries to the act of entering into possession of the truth – a truth we will prudently take down in our notes so that there will be no risk of its escaping us – it would be ungrateful to complain of the difficulties these labours give us, for the calm and the cool air are so exquisite, in the old convent where the nuns still wear the high hennins with white wings that they have on their heads in the Roger van der Weyden painting in the locutory, and, while we work, the seventeenth-century bells so tenderly take the chill out of the ingenuous water of the canal that a little pale sun is enough to dazzle us between the double row of trees, bare of leaves since the end of summer, that brush the mirrors affixed to the gabled houses on either side.[9]

This conception of a truth that is deaf to the call of reflection and amenable to the play of external influences, a truth which can be obtained through letters of introduction, which can be placed in our hands by someone who physically possesses it (without, perhaps, understanding it), which lets

9. I need not add that it would be fruitless to look for this convent near Utrecht and that this entire passage is pure imagination. It was, however, suggested to me by the following passage in Léon Séché's book on Sainte-Beuve: 'One day, while at Liège, he [Sainte-Beuve] took it into his head to make the acquaintance of the little church in Utrecht. It was rather late, but Utrecht lay at quite a distance from Paris and I do not know if his *Volupté* would have been enough to open the gates of the Amersfoort archives to him. I rather doubt it, for even after the first two volumes of his *Port-Royal*, the pious scholar who guarded these archives at the time had [etc.] Sainte-Beuve obtained from the good Abbé Karsten, not without difficulty, permission to half-open some of the cardboard boxes and peek inside... Open the second edition of *Port-Royal* and you will find Sainte-Beuve's acknowledgment of Karsten' (Léon Séché, *Sainte-Beuve*, vol. I, pp. 229 ff.). As for the details of the trip, they are all based on real impressions. I do not know if you do pass through Dordrecht to get to Utrecht, but Dordrecht is described here just as I saw it. It was while going to Vollendam, not to Utrecht, that I traveled in a horse-drawn barge between the reeds. The canal that I placed in Utrecht is in Delft. It was at the Hôpital de Bon-Dieu in Beaune that I saw the Roger van der Weyden painting and the nuns belonging to, I think, a Flemish order, who still wear the headdresses not of the van der Weyden but of other paintings I saw in Holland.

itself be copied into a notebook – this conception of truth is still far from the most dangerous one. Because, very often, for the historian and even for the scholar, this truth that they seek at a distance, in a book, is properly speaking less the truth itself than a sign or a proof, something that therefore makes way for another truth that it suggests or verifies, and this latter truth at least is an individual creation of his spirit. It is not the same for a literary man. He reads for the sake of reading, to store up what he has read. For him the book is not an angel who takes flight as soon as he has opened the gates of the heavenly garden, but an idol, unmoving, worshipped for its own sake, that communicates a fake dignity to everything around it instead of receiving a true dignity from the thoughts it awakens. The literary reader appeals to this fake dignity with a smile, in honour of some name that can be found in Villehardouin or Boccaccio,[10] in admiration of a custom described in Virgil. His spirit lacks all original activity and does not know how to isolate in books the substance which could make it stronger; he weighs himself down with the book as a whole, which instead of being something he can assimilate, a life principle, is for him a foreign body, a death principle. Need I add that if I describe this taste, this kind of fetishistic reverence for books, as unhealthy and pernicious, it is only relative to the ideal habits of a spirit altogether lacking in faults, one which does not exist; I do so like the physiologists who describe as an organ's normal function

10. Pure snobbery is more innocent. To take pleasure in someone's company because he had an ancestor in the Crusades is vanity, and intelligence has nothing to do with it, but to take pleasure in someone's company because his grandfather's name is mentioned often in Alfred de Vigny or in Chateaubriand, or because – a truly irresistible seduction for me, I must admit – her family's coat of arms is in the great rose window of Notre-Dame of Amiens (and I am thinking of a woman well worth our admiration without that fact): that is where intellectual sin begins. However, I have analysed this phenomenon at too great length elsewhere (although there is much that remains for me to say) to need to insist on it further here.

something which is hardly ever found in living beings. In real life, on the other hand, where there are no perfect spirits any more than there are entirely healthy bodies, those whom we call the great minds are as vulnerable to this 'literary sickness' as anyone else. More than anyone else, one might say. The taste for books seems to grow as intelligence grows, a bit lower down but on the same stalk, the way every passion is accompanied by a predilection for whatever surrounds the object of that passion, whatever is connected to it, whatever speaks of it in its absence. So too, the greatest writers, in the hours when they are not in direct communication with their thoughts, enjoy the company of books. Besides, is it not for them above all that the books were written? Do the books not reveal to them a thousand beauties which remain hidden from the masses? But the fact that some superior minds are what we call bookish does not in the slightest prove that this bookishness is not a defect. One cannot conclude from the fact that second-rate men are often hard-working and intelligent men often lazy that work is not a better mental discipline than laziness. Even so, to encounter one of our own flaws in a great man always makes us tempted to wonder if this flaw might not be at bottom an unrecognised virtue; it is not without pleasure that we learn that Victor Hugo knew Quintus-Curtius, Tacitus, and Justinian by heart, and that if anyone challenged him on the validity of a term he could trace its genealogy all the way back to its origins, citing quotations which demonstrated a true erudition.[11] (I have shown elsewhere how this erudition could nourish his genius instead of stifling it, the way a bundle of sticks can put out a small fire but feed a large one.) Maeterlinck, who for me is the opposite of a 'literary man' in this sense, whose spirit is constantly open to the thousand nameless emotions communicated by the beehive, the soil, or the grass, greatly reassures us about the dangers of erudition, of bibliophilia almost, when he describes for us as an

11. Paul Stapher, 'Memories of Victor Hugo', in the *Revue de Paris*.

amateur the engravings which adorn an old edition of Jacob Cats or Antonius Sanderus. Furthermore, since the dangers of erudition, when they do exist, threaten the intelligence much less than they do the sensibility, thinkers have a much greater capacity for productive reading (if one may put it this way) than creative writers. Schopenhauer, for example, gives us the picture of a mind energetic enough to wear lightly the most enormous erudition; each new piece of knowledge is immediately reduced to its core of reality, to the living portion it contains.

Schopenhauer never offers an opinion without immediately supporting it with multiple quotations, but we can feel that for him the texts he cites are only examples, unconscious anticipatory allusions in which he is happy to recognise certain aspects of his own thought but which in no way inspired it. I recall a passage of *The World as Will and Representation* where there are maybe twenty citations in a row. The topic is pessimism (and naturally I condense the quotations here): 'Just as in *Candide* Voltaire in his facetious manner wages war on optimism, so has Byron done the same, in his tragic way, in *Cain*. Herodotus reports that the Thracians welcomed the new-born child with lamentation and rejoiced at every death. This runs as follows in a fine verse preserved for us by Plutarch: '*Lugere genitum, tanta qui intravit mala...*' It is to this that we must attribute the Mexican custom of wishing [etc.], and in pursuance of the same feeling, Swift (if the biography by Sir Walter Scott is to be believed) early adopted the custom of celebrating his day of birth as a day of sadness. Well known is the passage in *Apology* where Plato says that death is a wonderful gain. A saying of Heraclitus shares the same conception: '*Vitæ nomen quidem est vita, opus autem mors.*' The fine lines of Theognis are well known: '*Optima sort homini non esse...*' Sophocles, in *Oedipus at Colonnus* (1224), gives the following abbreviation of this: '*Natum non esse sortes vincit alias omnes...*' Euripides says: '*Omnis hominum vita est plena dolore*' (*Hippolytus*

189), and Homer already said: '*Non enim quidquam alicubi est calamitosius homine omnium, quotquot super terram spirant...*' Even Pliny says: '*Nullum melius esse tempestiva morte.*' Shakespeare puts into the mouth of the old King Henry IV the words: 'O, if this were seen – The happiest youth / Would shut the book and sit him down and die.' Finally, Byron: ''Tis something better not to be.' Balthasar Gracián also brings before our eyes the misery of our existence in the darkest colours in the *Criticón*, etc. etc.'[12] If I had not already let myself run on far too long with Schopenhauer, I would have enjoyed completing this little demonstration with the aid of *Aphorisms on the Wisdom of Life*, which is perhaps, of all the works I know, the one which presupposes in its author the greatest originality along with the widest reading, such that, at the start of the book, every page of which contains numerous quotations, Schopenhauer was right to have written in all seriousness: 'Compilation is not my business.'

There is no doubt that friendship, friendship for individuals, is a frivolous thing, and reading is a friendship. But at least it is a sincere form of friendship, and the fact that it is directed at someone dead, someone absent, gives it something disinterested, almost touching. It is also a form of friendship unencumbered with everything that makes other friendships ugly. Since we all, we the living, are nothing but the dead who have not yet taken up our offices, all the courtesies, all the greetings in the entrance-hall, that we call respect, gratitude, and devotion and into which we mix so many lies, are unproductive and exhausting. Furthermore, from our first bonds of sympathy, admiration, and recognition, the first words we speak and the first letters we write weave around us the first threads of a web of habit, a veritable mode of existence which we can no longer extricate ourselves from in the ensuing

12. Schopenhauer, *The World as Will and Representation*, the chapter 'On the Vanity and Suffering of Life'.

33

friendships; not to mention that the excessive words we utter during this time remain, like promissory notes we have to pay, or else we will pay far more, for the rest of our lives, in self-reproach for having refused to honour them. In reading, friendship is suddenly returned to its initial purity. With books there is no civility. If we spend the evening with these friends, it is because we truly want to. From them, at least, we often part only with reluctance. And with none of the thoughts, when we have left them, that spoil other friendships: What did they think of us? Were we impolite? Did they like us? And the fear of being forgotten for someone else. All of these turmoils of friendship come to an end at the threshold of the pure and calm friendship of reading. No respectful deference either: we laugh at what Molière says only to the precise extent to which we find it funny; when he bores us we are not afraid to look bored; and when we have definitely had enough of him we put him back on the shelf as abruptly as if he were not a famous genius. The atmosphere of this pure form of friendship is a silence purer than words. For we speak for others, but keep silent for ourselves. Silence, too, does not carry the trace of our flaws, our hypocrisies, as words do. It is pure, it is an atmosphere in the truest sense. It does not interpose between the author's thought and our own the unavoidable obstacle, resistant to thought, of our different egos. Even the language of the book is pure (in any book worthy of the name), rendered transparent by the author's thought which has removed from the book everything that is not itself until the book becomes its faithful portrait; every sentence, fundamentally, is like every other, because they have all been spoken with the unique inflection of a single personality; there is thus a kind of con-tinuity, incompatible with the interactions we have in life and with everything foreign to thought that those interactions mix into it, a continuity which instantly enables us to follow the true line of the author's thought, the features of his physio-gnomy, as reflected in this tranquil mirror. We can delight in one feature after another of each of these authors without needing them to be worthy, because it is a great spiritual pleasure to discern these profound depictions and to love them, in a friendship without ego, without fine phrases, as if inside ourselves. Someone like Gautier, for example, pleases us as an ordinary good fellow with excellent taste (it is amusing to think that anyone could consider him a representative of artistic perfection). We do not exaggerate his spiritual capacities; in his *A Romantic in Spain*, where every sentence, when he least suspects it, accentuates and extends this line full of the grace and cheerfulness of his personality (the words fall into place of their own accord to trace it, because it is his personality that chose and arranged them), we cannot help but consider far removed from true art the compulsion he seems to feel not to let a single form or shape go by without describing it in its entirety, and adding a comparison that, because it is not born of a strong and pleasing impression, does not charm us in the least. We can only blame the pitiful aridity of his imagination when he compares the landscape with its various crops to 'those tailors' cards on which are stuck patterns of trousers and waistcoats', or when he says that there is nothing worth seeing on the journey from Paris to Angoulême. And we smile at this fervent admirer of the Gothic who, while in Chartres, does not even bother to go see the cathedral.[13]

But what good humor, what good taste! As we willingly follow this companion so full of high spirits on his adventures; he is so likeable that everything around him becomes likeable too. After the few days he spends with Captain Lebarbier de Tinan, delayed aboard his fine vessel 'glittering like gold' by a storm, we are sad that he says not a word more about this amiable seaman and makes us bid him farewell forever without telling us

13. 'I regret having passed through Chartres without being able to see the cathedral' (*A Romantic in Spain*, p. 4).

what became of him.[14] We can tell perfectly well that the cheerful braggadocio, the melancholy fits too, are in his case the somewhat bohemian habits of the journalist. But we pass over all of these faults, we do what he wants, we are entertained when he comes home soaked to the skin and dying of hunger and sleeplessness, and we are sad when he lists with a newspaper feuilletonist's sadness the names of the men of his generation who have died before their time. I was saying about him that his sentences sketch out his features, but when he least suspects it: for when words are chosen not by our mind pursuing its innermost affinities but by our desire to portray ourselves, then they will represent that desire, not our self. Fromentin, or Musset, despite all their gifts, left very second-rate portraits of themselves to posterity precisely because a portrait is what they wanted to leave; even so, they still interest us greatly, because their failure is instructive. So even when a book is not the mirror of a strong individual personality, it still reflects interesting intellectual defects. Bent over a book by Fromentin or one by Musset, we perceive at the core of the former how limited and foolish 'distinction' is, and at the core of the latter the emptiness of eloquence.

If the taste for books grows with intelligence, its dangers, as we have seen, decrease with intelligence. An original mind knows how to subordinate reading to its own individual activity. For such a mind, reading is nothing more than the noblest of distractions, and above all the most ennobling, because only reading and knowledge can teach us the 'good manners' of the mind. We can develop the strength of our sensibility and our intelligence only within ourselves, in the depths of our inner life, but it is through the contact with other minds which constitutes

14. He would later become, I am told, the celebrated admiral de Tinan, father of that Madame Pochet de Tinan whose name remains dear to artists, and grandfather of the brilliant cavalry officer. It was also he who, I believe, was in charge of supplies and communications between Francois II and the Queen of Naples before Gaeta. See Pierre de la Gorce, *History of the Second Empire*.

reading that our minds are 'fashioned.' Literary men remain, despite everything, the intellectual aristocracy, and not to know a certain book, a certain fact about the world of literature, will always be, even in a man of genius, a sign of intellectual commonness. Distinction and nobility – in the realm of the mind as well – consist in a sort of freemasonry of secret signs, and in having inherited certain traditions.[15]

In their taste for and enjoyment of reading, great writers are very quickly drawn to the classic books. Even those who seemed most 'romantic' to their contemporaries read hardly anything but the 'classics'. When Victor Hugo speaks in conversation about his reading, the names which come up the most often are Molière, Horace, Ovid, Regnard. Alphonse Daudet, the least bookish of writers, whose work is so full of modernity and vitality that it seems to have rejected the entire classical heritage, has ceaselessly read, quoted, and commented on Pascal, Montaigne, Diderot, Tacitus.[16] One might almost go so far as to say –

15. True distinction, moreover, always purports to address itself only to those men and women of distinction familiar with the same customs; it does not 'explain'. A book by Anatole France implies a mass of scholarly knowledge and makes constant allusions that the masses do not perceive, which produce, above and beyond the book's other beauties, its incomparable nobility.
16. This is no doubt why, when a great artist writes criticism, he often writes about new editions of older works, and very rarely about contemporary books. For example, Sainte-Beuve's *Monday Conversations* or Anatole France's *On Life and Letters*. But while Anatole France judges his contemporaries to perfection, Sainte-Beuve may rightly be said to have misjudged all the great writers of his time. And one cannot object that he was blinded by personal animosities: after having belittled Stendhal as a novelist to an unbelievable degree, he celebrates, as though in compensation, the man's modesty and discreet behavior, as if there were nothing else good to say about him! This blindness in Sainte-Beuve about his own era forms a strange contrast with his claims to clairvoyance and prescience: 'Everyone in the world is in a position to pass judgment on Racine and Bossuet,' he says in *Chateaubriand and His Literary Milieu*, 'but the sagacity of the judge and the perspicacity of the critic prove themselves above all upon new writing, as yet untried by the public. To judge at first sight, to divine, to lead the way – that is the critic's gift. How few possess it.'

reviving, perhaps, with this in any case quite partial interpretation, the old distinction between Classic and Romantic – that it is the public (the intelligent public, of course) who are romantic, while the masters (even the masters called romantic, the masters preferred by the romantic public) are classical. (This remark can be extended to all the arts. The public goes to hear the music of Vincent d'Indy; Vincent d'Indy studies his Monsigny.[17] The public goes to see Vuillard and Denis exhibits while Vuillard and Denis go to the Louvre.) This results, no doubt, from the fact that contemporary ideas, which original writers and artists make accessible and desirable to the public, are to a certain extent so much a part of them that a different idea is more diverting. This different idea demands of them, in order for them to approach it, more effort, and thus also gives them more pleasure; we always like to go outside ourselves a little, to travel, when we read.

17. And, conversely, classical writers have no better commentators than the 'romantics.' Only the romantics know how to read classical works because they read them the way they were written, romantically; because to read a poet or prose writer well one must be, oneself, not a scholar but a poet or writer. This is true of the least 'romantic' works. It was not the rhetoric professors who drew our attention to Boileau's beautiful lines, but Victor Hugo:

> *Et dans quatre mouchoirs de sa beauté salis*
> *Envoie au blanchisseur ses roses et ses lys.*

> [And in four handkerchiefs smeared with her beauties
> She sends to the laundry her roses and lilies.]

Or Anatole France:

> *L'ignorance et l'erreur à ses naissantes pièces*
> *En habits de marquis, en robes de comtesses.*

> [Ignorance and lapses in his newborn plays,
> In the cloaks of the marquis, the robes of the countess.]

– While I am correcting the proofs of this book, the most recent issue of *La Renaissance latine* (15 May 1905) gives me the opportunity to extend this remark to the fine arts with an additional example. The article by Mauclair demonstrates that the truest analysis of Greek statuary is that of Rodin.

But there is another reason to which, in conclusion, I would like to attribute this predilection that great minds have for older works.[18] Namely, that they contain more than just the beauty which the spirit that created them put into them. Contemporary works have that, but older works have received another, still more moving beauty from the fact that their very material, I mean the language in which they were written, is like a mirror held up to life. A little of the happiness we feel in walking around a city like Beaune, which preserves intact its fifteenth-century hospital complete with well, wash-house, vault of painted and paneled timber, the roof with high gables pierced by dormer windows and crowned with delicate spikes of hammered iron – everything there that the age left behind, so to speak, when it disappeared; all the things that must have belonged to that age alone, since none of the ages that followed witnessed the birth of anything like them – we feel a little of that happiness again when we wander in a tragedy by Racine or a volume by Saint-Simon. For they contain all the beautiful, obsolete forms of language which preserve the memory of usages and ways of feeling that no longer exist, enduring traces of a past unlike anything in the present, whose colours only time, in passing over them, has been able to enhance.

A tragedy by Racine, a volume of Saint-Simon's memoirs, is like those beautiful things which are made no longer. The language in which they were cast by the great artists, with a freedom that makes their sweetness shine and their native force stand out, moves us like the sight of certain kinds of marble, no longer in use today but used often by the workmen of the past. There is no question that the stone in these old buildings has

18. They themselves generally believe that this predilection is fortuitous – they assume that the most beautiful books simply happen, by chance, to have been written by older authors. And of course this may be true, because the older books we still read have been selected from the entirety of the past, so enormous compared to our contemporary age. But an accidental and arbitrary reason like this is not enough to explain such a general cast of mind.

faithfully preserved the sculptor's thought, but the sculptor has also preserved for us the stone of a type unknown today, clothed it in all the colours he knew how to draw from it, bring out, and harmonise. It is likewise the living syntax of seventeenth-century France – and in it vanished customs and turns of thought – that we love to find in Racine's poetry. The forms themselves of this syntax, laid bare, honoured, embellished by a chisel as sturdy as it is delicate, are what move us in his turns of phrase, colloquial to the point of strangeness and daring,[19] whose abrupt pattern we see, in the sweetest and most touching passages, flash by like an arrow or turn back in beautiful broken lines. It is these bygone forms, taken from the very life of the past, that we go to see in the works of Racine, as though in an ancient city preserved

---

19. For example, I believe that the charm we are accustomed to find in these line from Racine's *Andromaque*:

> *Pourquoi l'assassiner ? Qu'a-t-il fait ? A quel titre ?*
> *Qui te l'a dit ?*

> [Why murder him? What did he do? On what grounds?
> Who told you that?]

comes precisely from intentionally breaking the customary syntactical connections. 'On what grounds?' refers not to 'What did he do?' – the immediately preceding sentence – but to 'Why murder him?' and 'Who told you that?' refers to the 'murder' as well. (Recalling another line of Andromache's, '*Qui vous l'a dit, seigneur, qu'il me méprise ?*' ['Who told you that, milord, that he mistrusts me?'], we might at first suppose that 'Who told you that?' means 'Who told you to murder him?') Such zigzags of expression (the broken lines I speak of in the text above) can only obscure the meaning, and in fact I have heard a great actress, more concerned with clarity of sense than prosodic exactitude, simply say: 'Why murder him? On what grounds? What did he do?' Racine's most famous lines are in reality famous because we are charmed by their bold audacity of language, thrown like a daring bridge from one euphonious riverbank to the other. '*Je t'aimais inconstant,* qu'aurais-je fait *fidèle*' ['I loved you faithlessly, *what would I have done* faithful']. Such pleasure we get from the beautiful encounters of these phrases, whose almost commonplace simplicity gives their meaning, as in certain faces in paintings by Mantegna, such sweet fullness, such beautiful colours:

intact. We feel the same emotion before these forms of language as we feel before equally obsolete forms of architecture; them, too, we can admire only in the rare and magnificent examples that the past which made them has bequeathed to us: the old city walls, the castle keeps, the towers, the baptisteries of the churches; the little cemetery, near the cloister or under the ossuary Atrium, in which rest forgotten, in the sun, beneath its butterflies and its flowers, the funerary Fountain and the Lantern of the Dead.

Furthermore, it is not only the sentences and phrases which sketch out before our eyes the olden shapes of the soul. Between the phrases – I am thinking here of the very old books, which were originally read out loud – in the intervals which separate

> *Et dans un fol amour ma jeunesse* embarquée…
> [And *set sail* on mad, youthful love…]
>
> *Réunissons trois cœurs qui n'ont pu* s'accorder.
> [Let us unite three hearts that could not *agree*.]

This is why one should read the actual texts of classical writers, and not be satisfied with excerpts or selections. Writers' most famous pages are often those where this inner structure of their language is masked by the beauty of the excerpt, beauty of an almost universal character. I do not think that the particular essence of Gluck's music is as apparent in his sublime melodies as in the cadenzas of his recitatives, whose harmonic movement is like the sound of his genius' own voice as it involuntarily falls back, every time you hear it as it were catch its breath, into an intonation that displays all his naive gravity and refinement. Anyone who has seen photographs of Saint Mark's in Venice (and I am speaking here only of the exterior of the monument) may think he has an idea of this domed church, but it is only by approaching the multicolored curtain of its cheerful columns until you can touch them with your hand, only by seeing the strange and solemn power that has curled the leaves and perched birds on the capitals you can distinguish only from up close, only by being in the square itself and receiving the impression of the low-set monument, the full length of its façade with its flowered columns and its festive decoration, its look of a building in a World's Fair, that you can feel its true, complex individuality blaze forth from these details full of significance but secondary and impossible for any photograph to capture.

them, there remains, even now, as in an undefiled hypogeum, filling up all the interstices, a silence many centuries old. Often, in the Gospel of St Luke, coming across the *two dots of ink* which interrupt it before each of the almost song-like passages with which it is strewn,[20] I have heard the silence of the worshipper who has just stopped reading out loud in order to intone the verses that follow[21] like a psalm that reminds him of the oldest psalms in the Bible. This silence still fills the pause in the sentence which, having divided itself in two to enclose that silence, preserved its shape; more than once, while I read, it carried to me the scent of a rose which the breeze coming in through the open window had spread throughout the upper chamber that held the Assembly, a scent which has not dispersed for seventeen hundred years.

How many times, in the *Divine Comedy*, in Shakespeare, have I had the impression of coming face to face with a little of the past inserted into an hour of the present – the same dreamlike impression you have in Venice, on the Piazzetta, before the two grey and pink granite columns which bear atop their Greek capitals the Lion of St Mark on one, Saint Theodore treading upon the crocodile on the other: two handsome foreigners from the East, come from across the same sea that they now watch from a distance, the sea that comes to die at their feet. Both of them, without understanding the conversations conducted around them in a language different

20. 'And Mary said: "My soul doth magnify the Lord, and my spirit hath rejoiced in God my Savior"'; 'And his father Zacharias was filled with the Holy Ghost, and prophesied, saying: "Blessed be the Lord God of Israel; for he hath visited and redeēmed his people"'; 'Then took he him up in his arms, and blessed God, and said: "Lord, now lettest thou thy servant depart in peace"' etc.
21. In truth, no positive evidence permits me to assert that the giver of these lectures sang the kind of psalms that Saint Luke inserted in his gospel. But it seems clear enough to me from the juxtaposition of different passages in Renan's *Origins of Christianity*, especially *Saint Paul*, pp. 257 ff.; *Apostles*, pp. 99 and 100; and *Marcus Aurelius*, pp. 502, 503, etc.

from that of their homeland, on this public square where their remote and distracted smile still glitters, continue to prolong among us their days from the twelfth century that they have intercalated into our days of today. Yes, in the middle of this public square, in the midst of the present day whose reign it here interrupts, a little of the twelfth century, vanished so long ago, rises up in a thin double surge of pink granite. Everywhere around us, the present days – the days we live – circulate, crowd around the columns, buzz with activity but then suddenly stop and take flight like bees we have brushed aside, for those high, thin storehouses of the past are not in the present, they are in another time into which the present cannot penetrate. All around those pink columns that shoot up toward their broad capitals, the days of the present crowd and buzz, but the columns inserted among them brush them aside, defining with their slender impenetrability the inviolable terrain of the Past:– a Past which has surged familiarly into the midst of the present, which has the slightly unreal look of things that a kind of illusion makes us see as though they were a few steps away when in fact they are many centuries away; their whole appearance aimed a bit too directly at the mind, exalting it a little, as one would expect from a ghost arisen from a buried time; nonetheless there, in our midst, approachable, crowded round, felt, unmoving, in the sun.

Lecture I — Sesame. Of Kings' Treasuries by John Ruskin, Notes by Marcel Proust

You shall each have a cake of sesame,—and ten pound.

– Lucian: *The Fisherman*[1]

1. My first duty this evening is to ask your pardon for the ambiguity of title under which the subject of lecture has been announced: for indeed I am not going to talk of kings, known as regnant, nor of treasuries, understood to contain wealth; but of quite another order of royalty, and another material of riches, than those usually acknowledged. I had even intended to ask your attention for a little while on trust, and (as sometimes one contrives, in taking a friend to see a favourite piece of scenery)

1. This epigraph, which did not appear in the first editions of *Sesame and Lilies*, casts a supplemental ray of light that not only reaches the last sentence of the lecture (see p. 93) but retrospectively illuminates everything that precedes that sentence. Having given his lecture the symbolic title of 'Sesame' (the 'Sesame' of the *Thousand and One Nights* – the magic word which opens the door to the thieves' cave – as an allegory of reading, which opens for us the door of those treasuries where the most valuable wisdom of men is stored up: books), Ruskin amused himself by taking up the word 'sesame' for its own sake and, irrespective of the two meanings it has here (Ali Baba's 'Open Sesame' and reading), insisting on its original meaning (sesame seeds) and further embellishing it with a quotation from Lucian, playing a sort of game with the word by making the original significance appear sharply under the conventional meaning that the word has for the Arabian storyteller and for Ruskin. In truth, Ruskin thereby raises by a degree the symbolic significance of his title, because the quotation from Lucian reminds us that 'sesame' was already deflected from its true meaning in the *Thousand and One Nights*, thus its meaning as the title of Ruskin's lecture is as an allegory of allegory. The quotation clearly expresses, at the outset, the three meanings of the word 'sesame': reading which opens the gates of wisdom, Ali Baba's magic word, and the enchanted grain. Thus, from the beginning, Ruskin lays out his three themes and at the end of the lecture he will inextricably blend them

to hide what I wanted most to show, with such imperfect cunning as I might, until we unexpectedly reached the best point of view by winding paths. But – and as also I have heard it said, by men practised in public address, that hearers are never so much fatigued as by the endeavour to follow a speaker who gives them no clue to his purpose,– I will take the slight mask off at once, and tell you plainly that I want to speak to you about the treasures hidden in books; and about the way we find them, and the way we lose them. A grave subject, you will say; and a wide one! Yes; so wide that I shall make no effort to touch the compass of it. I will try only to bring before you a few simple thoughts about reading, which press themselves upon me every day more deeply,[2] as I watch the course of the public mind with respect to our daily enlarging means of education; and the answeringly wider spreading on the levels, of the irrigation of literature.

together, in the last sentence whose final chord will recall the tones of the opening (the grains of sesame) and take from these three themes – or rather five, the two others being 'Kings' Treasuries' in the symbolic sense of books, and the different Kings with their different kinds of treasuries, a new theme introduced toward the end of the lecture – an extraordinary richness and plenitude.

At various times, Ruskin tried out as many as five epigraphs for the 'Sesame' lecture, and if, in the end, he opted for the quotation from Lucian, it was no doubt because, precisely by lying farther from the sentiments of the lecture than the others, it added more, provided more embellishment, and best shed light on the various symbols by rejuvenating the meaning of the word 'sesame'. It doubtless also served to bring the treasures of wisdom into line with the charm of a frugal life, and give to his advice for individual wisdom the additional range of maxims on social happiness. This last intention becomes clearer toward the middle of the lecture. But it is precisely the attraction of Ruskin's work that between the various ideas in a given book, and between the different books, there are connections which he does not make explicit, which he lets appear just barely, for an instant, and which in any case may have been linked together only after the fact but which are never artificial because they are always drawn from the always self-identical substance of his thought. The various but consistent preoccupations of this thought are what give these books a unity

2. It happens that I have practically some connection with schools for different classes of youth; and I receive many letters from parents respecting the education of their children. In the mass of these letters I am always struck by the precedence which the idea of a 'position in life' takes above all other thoughts in the parents' – more especially in the mothers' – minds. 'The education befitting such and such a *station in life*' – this is the phrase, this the object, always. They never seek, as far as I can make out, an education good in itself; even the conception of abstract rightness in training rarely seems reached by the writers. But, an education 'which shall keep a good coat on my son's back;– which shall enable him to ring with confidence the visitors' bell at double-belled doors; which shall result ultimately in establishment of a double-belled door to his own house;– in a word, which shall lead to advancement in life;– *this* we pray for on bent knees – and this is *all* we pray for.' It never

more real than the unity of composition, which, it must be said, his books often lack.

I see that in the note I have placed at the end of 'Of Kings' Treasuries', I claimed to have found seven themes in the last sentence. In reality, Ruskin takes all the main ideas – or images – which have come up, somewhat chaotically, during his lecture, and sets them next to each other, mixes them, manipulates them, makes them shine together. That is how he works. He moves from one idea to the next without any apparent order, but actually the imagination which leads him is following its own deep affinities and imposing a higher logic on him in spite of himself, to such an extent that at the end he finds himself to have obeyed a kind of secret plan, unveiled at the end, that retroactively imposes a kind of order on the whole and makes it seem magnificently staged, right up to the climax of the final apotheosis. However, even if the disorder is comparable in all of his books, they do not all make the same move of retaking the reins at the end and pretending to have controlled and guided his steeds all along. Here too we should not see it as anything but a game.

2. A very common idea in Ruskin. Cf. *St Mark's Rest:* 'No day of my life passes now to its sunset, without leaving me more doubtful of all our cherished contempts, etc. and more earnest to discover, etc…' (*St. Mark's Rest*, 'The Shrine of the Slaves') – and *passim* throughout his work.

seems to occur to the parents that there may be an education which, in itself, *is* advancement in Life;– that any other than that may perhaps be advancement in Death; and that this essential education might be more easily got, or given, than they fancy, if they set about it in the right way; while it is for no price, and by no favour, to be got, if they set about it in the wrong.

3. Indeed, among the ideas most prevalent and effective in the mind of this busiest of countries, I suppose the first – at least that which is confessed with the greatest frankness, and put forward as the fittest stimulus to youthful exertion – is this of 'Advancement in life'. May I ask you to consider with me, what this idea practically includes, and what it should include?

Practically, then, at present, 'advancement in life' means, becoming conspicuous in life; obtaining a position which shall be acknowledged by others to be respectable or honourable. We do not understand by this advancement, in general, the mere making of money, but the being known to have made it; not the accomplishment of any great aim, but the being seen to have accomplished it. In a word, we mean the gratification of our thirst for applause. That thirst, if the last infirmity of noble minds, is also the first infirmity of weak ones; and, on the whole, the strongest impulsive influence of average humanity: the greatest efforts of the race have always been traceable to the love of praise, as its greatest catastrophes to the love of pleasure.

4. I am not about to attack or defend this impulse. I want you only to feel how it lies at the root of effort; especially of all modern effort.[3] It is the gratification of vanity which is, with us, the stimulus of toil and balm of repose; so closely does it touch the very springs of life that the wounding of our vanity is always spoken of (and truly) as in its measure *mortal*; we call it 'mortification', using the same expression which we should apply to a gangrenous and incurable bodily hurt. And although a few of us may be physicians enough to recognise the various

3. Cf. the same idea in *Le Maître de la Mer* by Eugène-Melchior de Vogüé.

effect of this passion upon health and energy, I believe most honest men know, and would at once acknowledge, its leading power with them as a motive. The seaman does not commonly desire to be made captain only because he knows he can manage the ship better than any other sailor on board. He wants to be made captain that he may be *called* captain. The clergyman does not usually want to be made a bishop only because he believes that no other hand can, as firmly as his, direct the diocese through its difficulties. He wants to be made bishop primarily that he may be called 'My Lord'. And a prince does not usually desire to enlarge, or a subject to gain, a kingdom, because he believes no one else can as well serve the State, upon its throne; but, briefly, because he wishes to be addressed as 'Your Majesty', by as many lips as may be brought to such utterance.

5. This, then, being the main idea of 'advancement in life', the force of it applies, for all of us, according to our station, particularly to that secondary result of such advancement which we call 'getting into good society'. We want to get into good society, not that we may have it, but that we may be seen in it; and our notion of its goodness depends primarily on its conspicuousness.

Will you pardon me if I pause for a moment to put what I fear you may think an impertinent question? I never can go on with an address unless I feel, or know, that my audience are either with me or against me: I do not much care which, in beginning; but I must know where they are; and I would fain find out, at this instant, whether you think I am putting the motives of popular action too low. I am resolved, to-night, to state them low enough to be admitted as probable; for when-ever, in my writings on Political Economy, I assume that a little honesty, or generosity, – or what used to be called 'virtue', – may be calculated upon as a human motive of action, people always answer me, saying, 'You must not calculate on that: that is not in human nature: you must not assume anything to be common to men but acquisitiveness and jealousy; no other feeling ever has influence on them, except accidentally, and in matters out of the way of business.' I begin, accordingly, to-night low in the scale of motives; but I must know if you think me right in doing so. Therefore, let me ask those who admit the love of praise to be usually the strongest motive in men's minds in seeking advancement, and the honest desire of doing any kind of duty to be an entirely secondary one, to hold up their hands. *(About a dozen hands held up – the audience, partly, not being sure the lecturer is serious, and, partly, shy of expressing opinion.)* I am quite serious – I really do want to know what you think; however, I can judge by putting the reverse question. Will those who think that duty is generally the first, and love of praise the second, motive, hold up their hands? *(One hand reported to have been held up behind the lecturer.)* Very good: I see you are with me, and that you think I have not begun too near the ground. Now, without teasing you by putting farther question, I venture to assume that you will admit duty as at least a secondary or tertiary motive. You think that the desire of doing something useful, or obtaining some real good, is indeed an existent collateral idea, though a secondary one, in most men's desire of advancement. You will grant that moderately honest men desire place and office, at least in some measure for the sake of beneficent power;[4] and would wish to associate rather with sensible and well-informed persons than with fools

4. Cf. 'You may observe, as an almost unexceptional character in the "sagacious wisdom" of the Protestant clerical mind, that it instinctively assumes the desire of power and place not only to be universal in Priesthood, but to be always purely selfish in the ground of it. The idea that power might possibly be desired for the sake of its benevolent use, so far as I remember, does not once occur in the pages of any ecclesiastical historian of recent date.' *(The Bible of Amiens,* III.33)

5. Meanwhile, the continually observed fact that many people of modest background but distinguished by their talents are snobs simply means that they often forego the society of other talented people in order to seek out the company of 'ignorant and foolish' men whom they are happy to see and be seen with.

and ignorant persons, whether they are seen in the company of the sensible ones or not.[5] And finally, without being troubled by repetition of any common truisms about the preciousness of friends, and the influence of companions, you will admit, doubtless, that according to the sincerity of our desire that our friends may be true, and our companions wise,– and in proportion to the earnestness and discretion with which we choose both,– will be the general chances of our happiness and usefulness.

6. But, granting that we had both the will and the sense to choose our friends well, how few of us have the power! or, at least, how limited, for most, is the sphere of choice![6] Nearly all our associations are determined by chance or necessity; and restricted within a narrow circle. We cannot know whom we would; and those whom we know, we cannot have at our side when we most need them. All the higher circles of human intelligence are, to those beneath, only momentarily and partially open. We may, by good fortune, obtain a glimpse of a great poet, and hear the sound of his voice; or put a question

6. This idea seems to us very beautiful in truth because we can feel the spiritual use to which Ruskin is about to put it; we can feel that the 'friends' here are merely tokens, and through these friends whom we cannot choose we already sense, about to appear, the friends we can choose, the main characters of the lecture: books, who have not yet made their entrance, like the star actress who does not come on stage in the first act. And we can see this specious but nevertheless fair reasoning as a kind of Platonic argument, which Ruskin, the disciple and brother of Plato, elsewhere conducts so naturally: 'Still, Critias, you cannot choose your friends however you want…' But here – as so often elsewhere in the Greeks, who have said all the true things but have not sought out all the true, more hidden pathways connecting those things – the comparison is not convincing. For one *can* be in a situation in life which *does* permit one to choose the friends one wants (a situation in life combined, of course, with intelligence and charm, without which the people whom one might choose would not be one's *friends* in the true sense of the word, but in the end all these attributes *can* be found together; I do not say often, but it is enough that I can find a few examples in my own milieu). Even for these privileged

to a man of science, and be answered good-humouredly. We may intrude ten minutes' talk on a cabinet minister, answered probably with words worse than silence, being deceptive; or snatch, once or twice in our lives, the privilege of throwing a bouquet in the path of a princess, or arresting the kind glance of a queen. And yet these momentary chances we covet; and spend our years, and passions, and powers, in pursuit of little more than these; while, meantime, there is a society continually open to us, of people who will talk to us as long as we like, whatever our rank or occupation;– talk to us in the best words they can choose, and of the things nearest their hearts. And this society, because it is so numerous and so gentle, and can be kept waiting round us all day long,– kings and statesmen lingering patiently, not to grant audience, but to gain it! – in those plainly furnished and narrow ante-rooms, our bookcase shelves,– we make no account of that company,– perhaps never listen to a word they would say, all day long!

7. You may tell me, perhaps, or think within yourselves, that the apathy with which we regard this company of the noble,

beings, however, the friends they can choose at will cannot in any way take the place of books (which proves that books are not merely friends whom one can choose to be as wise as one wants), because in truth the essential difference between a book and a person is not the greater or lesser wisdom in one or the other but the way we communicate with them. Our mode of communication with people entails a loss of the active forces of our soul, while the wondrous miracle of reading on the other hand – communication in the bosom of solitude – concentrates and excites those forces. When you read, you receive another thought and are nonetheless alone, in the midst of your labour of thought, your aspiration, your personal activity: you receive another's ideas in your spirit, in other words you can truly become one with those ideas, you are this other person and yet you cannot help but develop your own self with greater variety than if you were thinking alone; you are driven by another along your own path. In conversation, even leaving aside the moral and social influences and the like which the presence of an interlocutor creates, communication takes place through the mediation of sounds, the spiritual blow is softened, inspiration and profound thought are impossible. What's more, thought is falsified when it becomes spoken

who are praying us to listen to them; and the passion with which we pursue the company, probably of the ignoble, who despise us, or who have nothing to teach us, are grounded in this,– that we can see the faces of the living men, and it is themselves, and not their sayings, with which we desire to become familiar. But it is not so. Suppose you never were to see their faces;– suppose you could be put behind a screen in the statesman's cabinet, or the prince's chamber, would you not be glad to listen to their words, though you were forbidden to advance beyond the screen? And when the screen is only a little less, folded in two instead of four, and you can be hidden behind the cover of the two boards that bind a book, and listen all day long, not to the casual talk, but to the studied, determined, chosen addresses of the wisest of men;– this station of audience, and honourable privy council, you despise!

8. But perhaps you will say that it is because the living people talk of things that are passing, and are of immediate interest to you, that you desire to hear them. Nay; that cannot be so, for the living people will themselves tell you about passing matters

---

thought, as proven by the superiority of writers over those who enjoy and excel too much in conversation. (Despite the illustrious exceptions one might cite here, despite the testimony of someone like Emerson himself, who attributes a true virtue of inspiration to conversation, we can say that in general conversation puts us on the path of brilliant formulations or pure arguments but almost never on the path of profound impressions.) Thus the graceful reason that Ruskin gives (the impossibility of choosing one's friends and the possibility of choosing one's books) is not the real reason. It is only a contingent reason – the real one is the essential difference between the two modes of communication. Again, the field from which one chooses one's friends may not be restricted; granted, even in that case it is restricted to the living, but even if all of the dead were still alive they would still only be able to converse with us the same way the living do, and a conversation with Plato would still be a conversation, that is, an exercise immeasurably more superficial than reading. The value of the things we hear or read are of far less importance than the inner state which they can create in us, which can be profound only in solitude, or in the populated solitude of reading.

much better in their writings than in their careless talk. Yet I admit that this motive does influence you, so far as you prefer those rapid and ephemeral writings to slow and enduring writings – books, properly so called. For all books are divisible into two classes, the books of the hour, and the books of all time. Mark this distinction – it is not one of quality only. It is not merely the bad book that does not last, and the good one that does. It is a distinction of species. There are good books for the hour, and good ones for all time; bad books for the hour, and bad ones for all time. I must define the two kinds before I go farther.

9. The good book of the hour, then,– I do not speak of the bad ones,– is simply the useful or pleasant talk of some person whom you cannot otherwise converse with, printed for you. Very useful often, telling you what you need to know; very pleasant often, as a sensible friend's present talk would be. These bright accounts of travels; good-humoured and witty discussions of question; lively or pathetic story-telling in the form of novel; firm fact-telling, by the real agents concerned in the events of passing history;—all these books of the hour, multiplying among us as education becomes more general, are a peculiar possession of the present age: we ought to be entirely thankful for them, and entirely ashamed of ourselves if we make no good use of them. But we make the worst possible use if we allow them to usurp the place of true books: for, strictly speaking, they are not books at all, but merely letters or newspapers in good print. Our friend's letter may be delightful, or necessary, to-day: whether worth keeping or not, is to be considered. The newspaper may be entirely proper at breakfast time, but assuredly it is not reading for all day. So, though bound up in a volume, the long letter which gives you so pleasant an account of the inns, and roads, and weather, last year at such a place, or which tells you that amusing story, or gives you the real circumstances of such and such events, how-ever valuable for occasional reference, may not be, in the real

sense of the word, a 'book' at all, nor, in the real sense, to be 'read'. A book is essentially not a talking thing, but a written thing;[7] and written, not with a view of mere communication, but of permanence. The book of talk is printed only because its author cannot speak to thousands of people at once; if he could, he would – the volume is mere *multiplication* of his voice. You cannot talk to your friend in India; if you could, you would; you write instead: that is mere *conveyance* of voice. But a book is written, not to multiply the voice merely, not to carry it merely, but to perpetuate it.[8] The author has something to say which he perceives to be true and useful, or helpfully beautiful. So far as he knows, no one has yet said it; so far as he knows, no one else can say it. He is bound to say it, clearly and melodiously if he may; clearly at all events. In the sum of his life he finds this to be the thing, or group of things, manifest to him;– this, the piece of true knowledge, or sight, which his share of sunshine and earth has permitted him to seize. He would fain set it down for ever; engrave it on rock, if he could; saying, 'This is the best of me; for the rest, I ate, and drank, and slept, loved, and hated, like another; my life was as the

7. This distinction exists, of course, in the theory I was just sketching out. A man can inspire us only if we hear him in solitude, that is, if we read him, but he must also have been inspired himself. Solitude only allows us to put ourselves into the state in which the author found himself, a state which could not have been produced if the book were a spoken book; one can no more read while speaking than write while speaking. In re-reading this sentence of Ruskin's, 'A book is not a talking thing, but a written thing', I feel as though I have contradicted him less than I thought. But in any case it must still be said that if a book is not a talking thing, but a written thing, it is also something read, not something listened to in conversation, and consequently it cannot be equated to a friend. If Ruskin did not say this, it is only because he was not trying to analyse the original state of soul of the *reader*.

8. 'To perpetuate' is there for the contrast. In reality, though, it is no longer the same voice that is to be perpetuated. If it were simply the same kind of voice – nothing but *spoken* words – then to perpetuate it would be as pointless as to carry it or multiply it.

vapour,[9] and is not; but this I saw and knew: this, if anything of mine, is worth your memory.' That is his 'writing'; it is, in his small human way, and with whatever degree of true inspiration is in him, his inscription, or scripture. That is a 'Book'.

10. Perhaps you think no books were ever so written?

But, again, I ask you, do you at all believe in honesty, or at all in kindness, or do you think there is never any honesty or benevolence in wise people? None of us, I hope, are so unhappy as to think that. Well, whatever bit of a wise man's work is honestly and benevolently done, that bit is his book or his piece of art.[10] It is mixed always with evil fragments – ill-done, redundant, affected work. But if you read rightly, you will easily discover the true bits, and those *are* the book.

9. James 4:14: 'For what is your life? It is even a vapour, that appeareth for a little time, and then vanisheth away.' Compare this with two beautiful adaptations of the same verse, first in *The Seven Lamps of Architecture:* 'and since our life must at the best be but a vapour that appears for a little time and then vanishes away, let it at least appear as a cloud in the height of Heaven, not as the thick darkness that broods over the blast of the Furnace, and rolling of the Wheel'; second in the third lecture of *Sesame and Lilies,* 'The Mystery of Life and Its Arts': 'whereas in earlier life, what little influence I obtained was due perhaps chiefly to the enthusiasm with which I was able to dwell on the beauty of the physical clouds, and of their colors in the sky; so all the influence I now desire to retain must be due to the earnestness with which I am endeavoring to trace the form and beauty of another kind of cloud than those; the bright cloud of which it is written – "What is your life? It is even as a vapor that appeareth for a little time, and then vanisheth away."' (§96)

10. Note this sentence carefully, and compare the *Queen of the Air*, §106. [Ruskin's note]

Here is the passage which Ruskin cites: 'Thus far of Abbeville building. Now I have here asserted two things,– first, the foundation of art in moral character; next, the foundation of morsal character in war. I must make both these assertions clearer, and prove them. First, of the foundation of art in moral character. Of course art-gift and amiability of disposition are two different things; a good man is not necessarily a painter, nor does an eye for colour necessarily imply an honest mind. But great art implies the union of both powers: it is the expression, by an art-gift, of a pure soul. If the gift is

11. Now books of this kind have been written in all ages by their[11] greatest men:– by great leaders, great statesmen, and great thinkers. These are all at your choice; and Life is short. You have heard as much before;– yet have you measured and mapped out this short life and its possibilities? Do you know, if you read this, that you cannot read that – that what you lose to-day you cannot gain to-morrow?[12] Will you go and gossip with your housemaid, or your stable-boy, when you may talk with queens and kings; or flatter yourself that it is with any worthy consciousness of your own claims to respect, that you jostle with the hungry and common crowd for *entrée* here, and audience there, when all the while this eternal court is open to you, with its society, wide as the world, multitudinous as its

not there, we can have no art at all; and if the soul – and a right soul too – is not there, the art is bad, however dexterous.' The opposite assertion (and these opposites may perhaps meet if one extends the two ideas, not all the way to infinity, but to a certain height) was expressed with extraordinary grace by Whistler in his *Ten O'Clock*. – Also recall the passage in *Stones of Venice* on an archivolt of St Mark's designed by an unknown artist: 'I believe the man who designed and delighted in that archivolt to have been wise, happy, and *holy*.'

11. This unusual use of the pronoun occurs often in Ruskin's work, e.g. *The Bible of Amiens* IV.23: 'These are the only two Bronze tombs of *her* Men of the great ages left in France.' Similarly in the subtitle of *The Bible of Amiens*: 'Sketches of the History of Christendom for Boys and Girls Who Have Been Held at *Its* Fonts.' Etc.

12. It was in obedience to an idea like this one that John Stuart Mill's father had him start learning Greek at the age of 3, and had him read, by age 8, all of Herodotus, Xenophon's *Cypropaedia* and *Memorabilia*, the *Lives* of Diogenes Laertius, part of Lucian, Isocrates, and six of Plato's dialogues, including the *Theatetus*. 'Through the early training bestowed on me by my father,' Mill says, 'I started with an advantage of a quarter of a century over my contemporaries.' We might oppose to this way of understanding our lives the beautiful *Essay* by Taine, where he shows that the hours of flânerie are the richest and most fruitful for the mind and spirit. And to go to the opposite extreme, we might find the way of life described so well by George Eliot in *Adam Bede* to be charming, even poetic, if not exactly profitable for the spirit (and besides, who knows, it might well be that too): 'Even idleness

days,[13] the chosen, and the mighty, of every place and time? Into that you may enter always; in that you may take fellowship and rank according to your wish; from that, once entered into it, you can never be outcast but by your own fault; by your aristocracy of companionship there, your own inherent aristocracy will be assuredly tested, and the motives with which you strive to take high place in the society of the living, measured, as to all the truth and sincerity that are in them, by the place you desire to take in this company of the Dead.[14]

12. 'The place you desire', and the place *you fit yourself for*, I must also say; because, observe, this court of the past differs from all living aristocracy in this:– it is open to labour and to merit, but to nothing else. No wealth will bribe, no name over-awe, no artifice deceive, the guardian of those Elysian gates. In the deep sense, no vile or vulgar person ever enters there.[15] At

is eager now – eager for art museums, periodical literature, and even scientific theorising and peeps through microscopes. Old Leisure was quite a different personage; he only read one newspaper, innocent of leaders… He lived chiefly in the country, among pleasant seats and homesteads, and was fond of sauntering by the fruit-tree wall, and scenting the apricots or sheltering himself under the orchard boughs. He knew nothing of week-day services, and thought none the worse of the Sunday sermon if it allowed him to sleep from the text to the blessing… He had an easy conscience… able to carry a great deal of beer or port wine – not being made squeamish by doubts and qualms and lofty aspirations… Fine old Leisure! Do not be severe upon him', etc. (*Adam Bede*, vol. 2, ch. 52.)

13. See note 11 above on Ruskin's use of this pronoun.

14. Actually the place we wish to occupy in the society of the dead in no way gives us the right to desire to occupy such a place in the society of the living. The virtue of the first ought to detach us from the second, and if reading and appreciation do not free us from ambition (I am speaking only of vulgar ambition, of course, what Ruskin calls 'the desire to have a good position in the world and in life'), it is a sophistry to say that we have gained through the former the right to succumb to the latter. A man is no more entitled to be 'received in good society', or to wish to be so received, just because he is more intelligent and cultured. This is one of those sophistries that the vanity of intelligent people seeks out in the arsenal of their intelligence in order to justify their basest inclinations.

the portières of that silent Faubourg St Germain, there is but brief question:– 'Do you deserve to enter? Pass. Do you ask to be the companion of nobles? Make yourself noble, and you shall be. Do you long for the conversation of the wise? Learn to understand it, and you shall hear it. But on other terms? – no. If you will not rise to us, we cannot stoop to you. The living lord may assume courtesy, the living philosopher explain his thought to you with considerate pain; but here we neither feign nor interpret; you must rise to the level of our thoughts if you would be gladdened by them, and share our feelings, if you would recognise our presence.'

13. This, then, is what you have to do, and I admit that it is much. You must, in a word, love these people, if you are to be among them. No ambition is of any use. They scorn your ambition. You must love them, and show your love in these two following ways.

(1) First, by a true desire to be taught by them, and to enter into their thoughts. To enter into theirs, observe; not to find your own expressed by them. If the person who wrote the book is not wiser than you, you need not read it; if he be, he will think differently from you in many respects.[16]

(2) Very ready we are to say of a book, 'How good this is – that's exactly what I think!' But the right feeling is, 'How strange that is! I never thought of that before, and yet I see it is true; or if I do not now, I hope I shall, some day.' But whether thus submissively or not, at least be sure that you go to the author to get at *his* meaning, not to find yours. Judge it

15. Cf. Emerson: 'It is with a good book as it is with good company. Introduce a base person among gentlemen; it is all to no purpose; he is not their fellow. Every society protects itself. The company is perfectly safe, and he is not one of them, though his body is in the room.'
16. This idea offends a very widely held preconception in us, one which may, in addition, be just as true as Ruskin's paradox. However, let us let Ruskin enjoy his theory and let us not be surprised that this man 'wiser than us' thinks 'differently from us.'

afterwards if you think yourself qualified to do so; but ascertain it first. And be sure, also, if the author is worth anything, that you will not get at his meaning all at once;– nay, that at his whole meaning you will not for a long time arrive in any wise. Not that he does not say what he means, and in strong words too; but he cannot say it all; and what is more strange, *will* not, but in a hidden way and in parables, in order that he may be sure you want it.[17] I cannot quite see the reason of this, nor analyse that cruel reticence in the breasts of wise men which makes them always hide their deeper thought.[18] They do not give it you by way of help, but of reward; and will make themselves sure that you deserve it before they allow you to reach it. But it is the same with the physical type of wisdom, gold. There seems, to you and me, no reason why the electric forces of the earth should not carry whatever there is of gold within it at once to the mountain tops, so that kings and people

17. Yet this type of fog that envelops the splendour of beautiful books, like the mist of a beautiful morning, is a natural fog, the breath so to speak of the genius who exhales it unconsciously, not an artificial veil that he voluntarily surrounds his writing with in order to hide it from the masses. When Ruskin says he 'wants to make sure that you are worthy of it', it is simply a figure of speech. For to give one's thought a brilliant form, more accessible and more seductive to the public, would diminish it – that is what an easy writer does, a writer of the second rank. But to envelop one's thought so that only those who take the trouble to lift the veil may understand it, that is what a difficult writer does, who is no less a writer of the second rank. The writer of the first rank is the one who uses whatever words are dictated to him by an interior necessity, by the vision of his thought which he cannot alter in the least – and uses those words without asking himself whether they please the masses or repel them. Sometimes the great writer feels that, instead of his sentences at the bottom of which flickers a faint uncertain light that not every gaze will perceive, he would like to be recognised as a great man (he need only array and display the delightful metals that he pitilessly melts down and makes disappear in the process of constructing his somber alloys), recognised by the crowd and, an even more diabolical temptation, by those of his friends who deny his genius, and most of all by his mistress. That is when he will write a second-rate book, with everything that is kept unrevealed in a beautiful

might know that all the gold they could get was there; and without any trouble of digging, or anxiety, or chance, or waste of time, cut it away, and coin as much as they needed. But Nature does not manage it so. She puts it in little fissures in the earth, nobody knows where: you may dig long and find none; you must dig painfully to find any.

14. And it is just the same with men's best wisdom. When you come to a good book, you must ask yourself, 'Am I inclined to work as an Australian miner would? Are my pickaxes and shovels in good order, and am I in good trim myself, my sleeves well up to the elbow, and my breath good, and my temper?' And, keeping the figure a little longer, even at cost of tiresomeness, for it is a thoroughly useful one, the metal you are in search of being the author's mind or meaning, his words are as the rock which you have to crush and smelt in order to get at it. And your pickaxes are your own care, wit, and learning; your

book, which makes up the noble atmosphere of silence, the wondrous veneer that sparkles with the sacrifice of everything left unsaid. Instead of writing Flaubert's *Sentimental Education* he will write Maupassant's *Strong as Death*. And it is not the desire to write *Sentimental Education* rather than the other kind of book which makes him renounce all these vain beauties, it is no consideration foreign to his work, no reasoning in which he says 'I'. *He* is only the site where the thoughts are formed which select themselves at every moment, which build and perfect the necessary and unique form in which they will be made incarnate.

18. It would be wrong to see in this the thinker's whim; on the contrary, that would detract from the depth of his thought. But the fact that to understand something is in a way, as we have said, to be equal to it, means that to understand a profound thought is to have, at the moment when we understand it, a profound thought of our own, and this demands some effort, a genuine descent into our own heart, passing through and leaving far behind us those clouds of ephemeral thought through which we are ordinarily content to view things. Only desire and love give us the strength to make this effort; the only books we incorporate into ourselves are those we read with a genuine appetite, after having struggled to procure them for ourselves, so great was our need for them.

smelting furnace is your own thoughtful soul. Do not hope to get at any good author's meaning without those tools and that fire; often you will need sharpest, finest chiselling, and patientest fusing, before you can gather one grain of the metal.

15. And, therefore, first of all, I tell you earnestly and authoritatively (I *know* I am right in this),[19] you must get into the habit of looking intensely at words, and assuring yourself of their meaning, syllable by syllable – nay, letter by letter. For though it is only by reason of the opposition of letters in the function of signs, to sounds in the function of signs, that the study of books is called 'literature', and that a man versed in it is called, by the consent of nations, a man of letters instead of a man of books, or of words, you may yet connect with that accidental nomenclature this real fact:[20]– that you might read all the books in the British Museum (if you could live long enough), and remain an utterly 'illiterate', uneducated person; but that if you read ten pages of a good book, letter by letter,– that is to say, with real accuracy,– you are for evermore in some measure an educated person. The entire difference between education and non-education (as regards the merely intellectual part of it), consists in this accuracy. A well-educated

19. Sometimes Ruskin gives profound advice without revealing his reason for giving it, the way a doctor cannot give a full physiological explanation to a patient in order to justify his prescription; it may seem arbitrary to the patient but another doctor, if you told him about it, would judge it to be quite correct.

20. Just as in *The Bible of Amiens* (II.1), we here see Ruskin asking us to connect certain important ideas to a 'purely formal and arithmetical' division (he says, it is true, 'formal and arithmetical at first sight' but it is not so only at first sight, it stays so throughout). In the same chapter (II.30 and 31) he connects all of his ideas about the Salian Franks to etymologies that are necessarily fanciful because of their sheer number: if any one of them were accurate (which is, in any case, highly unlikely), it would necessarily exclude the others. Finally, still in the same chapter II, he says: '*Fere-Encos* passing swiftly on the tongue into *Francos – a derivation surely not to be adopted*, but the idea it gives of a weapon is worth considering most carefully.'

gentleman may not know many languages,– may not be able to speak any but his own,– may have read very few books. But whatever language he knows, he knows precisely; whatever word he pronounces, he pronounces rightly; above all, he is learned in the *peerage* of words; knows the words of true descent and ancient blood, at a glance, from words of modern canaille; remembers all their ancestry, their intermarriages, distant relationships, and the extent to which they were admitted,[21] and offices they held, among the national noblesse of words at any time, and in any country. But an uneducated person may know, by memory, many languages, and talk them all, and yet truly know not a word of any,– not a word even of his own. An ordinarily clever and sensible seaman will be able to make his way ashore at most ports; yet he has only to speak a sentence of any language to be known for an illiterate person:[22] so also the accent, or turn of expression of a single sentence, will at once mark a scholar. And this is so strongly felt, so conclusively admitted, by educated persons, that a false accent or a mistaken syllable is enough, in the parliament of any civilized nation, to assign to a man a certain degree of inferior standing for ever.

21. Here the metaphor elevates the idea precisely with the aid of things whose stature Ruskin certainly would not recognise. The armorial probably meant nothing to him, and the type of people who know exactly whether a certain kind of person is *received* or *not received* (Balzac, *Gobseck*: 'Madame de Beauséant received her, it seems to me...' 'Yes, but only at her routs!' replied the vicountess.') – those who know the illustriousness of everyone's ancestry and intermarriages – must not have possessed in Ruskin's eyes a very enviable knowledge. Whether someone is of good blood or of obscure blood has little importance in a thinker's eyes. But Ruskin's image appeals to the idea that it has, on the contrary, great value: 'he knows the words of true descent and ancient blood...' So the pleasure that such images give the reader, and first of all gave the author, is in truth based on intellectual insincerity.
22. Someone I know sometimes tells her son: 'It would not matter to me in the least if you married a woman who had never heard of Ruskin, but I could not bear to see you marry a woman who said 'tram*v*ay" (instead of pronouncing it 'tram*w*ay').

16. And this is right; but it is a pity that the accuracy insisted on is not greater, and required to a serious purpose. It is right that a false Latin quantity should excite a smile in the House of Commons; but it is wrong that a false English *meaning* should *not* excite a frown there. Let the accent of words be watched; and closely: let their meaning be watched more closely still, and fewer will do the work. A few words well chosen, and distinguished, will do work that a thousand cannot, when every one is acting, equivocally, in the function of another. Yes; and words, if they are not watched, will do deadly work sometimes. There are masked words droning and skulking about us in Europe just now,– (there never were so many, owing to the spread of a shallow, blotching, blundering, infectious 'information', or rather deformation, everywhere, and to the teaching of catechisms and phrases at school instead of human meanings) – there are masked words abroad, I say, which nobody understands, but which everybody uses, and most people will also fight for, live for, or even die for, fancying they mean this or that, or the other, of things dear to them: for such words wear chameleon cloaks – 'ground-lion' cloaks,[23] of the colour of the ground of any man's fancy: on that ground they lie in wait, and rend them with a spring from it. There never were creatures of prey so mischievous, never diplomatists so cunning, never poisoners so deadly, as these masked words; they are the unjust stewards of all men's ideas: whatever fancy or favourite instinct a man most cherishes, he gives to his favourite masked word to take care of for him; the word at last comes to have an infinite power over him,– you cannot get at him but by its ministry.

17. And in languages so mongrel in breed as the English, there is a fatal power of equivocation put into men's hands, almost whether they will or no, in being able to use Greek or Latin words for an idea when they want it to be awful; and Saxon or otherwise common words when they want it to be vulgar. What a

23. An allusion to the etymology of 'chameleon': χαμαι λεον.

singular and salutary effect, for instance, would be produced on the minds of people who are in the habit of taking the Form of the 'Word' they live by, for the Power of which that Word tells them, if we always either retained, or refused, the Greek form 'biblos', or 'biblion', as the right expression for 'book' – instead of employing it only in the one instance in which we wish to give dignity to the idea, and translating it into English everywhere else. How wholesome it would be for many simple persons if, in such places (for instance) as Acts xix.19, we retained the Greek expression, instead of translating it, and they had to read – 'Many of them also which used curious arts, brought their bibles together, and burnt them before all men; and they counted the price of them, and found it fifty thousand pieces of silver'! Or if, on the other hand, we translated where we retain it, and always spoke of 'The Holy Book', instead of 'Holy Bible', it might come into more heads than it does at present, that the Word of God, by which the heavens were, of old, and by which they are now kept in store,[24] cannot be made a present of to anybody in morocco binding; nor sown on any wayside by help either of steam plough or steam press; but is nevertheless being offered to us daily, and by us with contumely refused; and sown in us daily, and by us, as instantly as may be, choked.

18. So, again, consider what effect has been produced on the English vulgar mind by the use of the sonorous Latin form 'damno', in translating the Greek κατακρίνω, when people charitably wish to make it forcible; and the substitution of the temperate 'condemn' for it, when they choose to keep it gentle; and what notable sermons have been preached by illiterate clergymen on – 'He that believeth not shall be damned'; though they would shrink with horror from translating Heb. xi.7, 'The saving of his house, by which he damned the world', or John

24. 2 Peter 3:5–7: 'Reserved unto fire against the day of judgment and perdition of ungodly men.'

viii.10–11, 'Woman, hath no man damned thee? She saith, No man, Lord. Jesus answered her, Neither do I damn thee: go and sin no more.' And divisions in the mind of Europe, which have cost seas of blood, and in the defence of which the noblest souls of men have been cast away in frantic desolation, countless as forest-leaves – though, in the heart of them, founded on deeper causes – have nevertheless been rendered practically possible, mainly, by the European adoption of the Greek word for a public meeting, 'ecclesia', to give peculiar respectability to such meetings, when held for religious purposes; and other collateral equivocations, such as the vulgar English one of using the word 'priest' as a contraction for 'presbyter'.

19. Now, in order to deal with words rightly, this is the habit you must form. Nearly every word in your language has been first a word of some other language – of Saxon, German, French, Latin, or Greek; (not to speak of eastern and primitive dialects). And many words have been all these – that is to say, have been Greek first, Latin next, French or German next, and English last: undergoing a certain change of sense and use on the lips of each nation; but retaining a deep vital meaning, which all good scholars feel in employing them, even at this day. If you do not know the Greek alphabet, learn it; young or old – girl or boy – whoever you may be,[25] if you think of reading seriously (which, of course, implies that you have some leisure at command), learn your Greek alphabet; then get good dictionaries of all these languages, and whenever you are in doubt about a word, hunt it down patiently. Read Max Müller's lectures thoroughly, to begin with; and, after that, never let a word escape you that looks suspicious. It is severe work; but you will find it, even at first, interesting, and at last endlessly amusing. And the general gain to your character, in power and precision, will be quite incalculable.

25. Cf. *The Bible of Amiens:* 'aimless – shall we say also, readers, young and old, travelling or abiding' (I, 5).

Mind, this does not imply knowing, or trying to know, Greek or Latin, or French. It takes a whole life to learn any language perfectly. But you can easily ascertain the meanings through which the English word has passed; and those which in a good writer's work it must still bear.

20. And now, merely for example's sake, I will, with your permission, read a few lines of a true book with you, carefully; and see what will come out of them. I will take a book perfectly known to you all. No English words are more familiar to us, yet few perhaps have been read with less sincerity. I will take these few following lines of 'Lycidas':–

Last came, and last did go,
The pilot of the Galilean lake.
Two massy keys he bore of metals twain,
(The golden opes, the iron shuts amain,)
He shook his mitred locks, and stern bespake,
'How well could I have spared for thee, young swain,
Enow of such as for their bellies' sake
Creep, and intrude, and climb into the fold!
Of other care they little reckoning make,
Than how to scramble at the shearers' feast,
And shove away the worthy bidden guest;
Blind mouths! that scarce themselves know how to hold
A sheep-hook, or have learn'd aught else, the least
That to the faithful herdman's art belongs!
What recks it them? What need they? They are sped;
And when they list, their lean and flashy songs
Grate on their scrannel pipes of wretched straw;
The hungry sheep look up, and are not fed,
But, swoln with wind, and the rank mist they draw,
Rot inwardly, and foul contagion spread;
Besides what the grim wolf with privy paw
Daily devours apace, and nothing said.'

Let us think over this passage, and examine its words.

First, is it not singular to find Milton assigning to St Peter, not only his full episcopal function, but the very types of it which Protestants usually refuse most passionately? His 'mitred' locks! Milton was no Bishop-lover; how comes St Peter to be 'mitred'? 'Two massy keys he bore.' Is this, then, the power of the keys claimed by the Bishops of Rome? and is it acknowledged here by Milton only in a poetical licence, for the sake of its picturesqueness, that he may get the gleam of the golden keys to help his effect?

Do not think it. Great men do not play stage tricks with the doctrines of life and death: only little men do that. Milton means what he says; and means it with his might too – is going to put the whole strength of his spirit presently into the saying of it. For though not a lover of false bishops, he *was* a lover of true ones; and the Lake-pilot is here, in his thoughts, the type and head of true episcopal power. For Milton reads that text, 'I will give unto thee the keys of the kingdom of heaven', quite honestly. Puritan though he be, he would not blot it out of the book because there have been bad bishops; nay, in order to understand *him*, we must understand that verse first; it will not do to eye it askance, or whisper it under our breath, as if it were a weapon of an adverse sect. It is a solemn, universal assertion, deeply to be kept in mind by all sects. But perhaps we shall be better able to reason on it if we go on a little farther, and come back to it. For clearly this marked insistence on the power of the true episcopate is to make us feel more weightily what is to be charged against the false claimants of episcopate; or generally, against false claimants of power and rank in the body of the clergy; they who, 'for their bellies' sake, creep, and intrude, and climb into the fold'.

21. Never think Milton uses those three words to fill up his verse, as a loose writer would.[26] He needs all the three;– especially those three, and no more than those– 'creep', and 'intrude', and 'climb'; no other words would or could serve the

turn, and no more could be added. For they exhaustively comprehend the three classes, correspondent to the three characters, of men who dishonestly seek ecclesiastical power. First, those who '*creep*' into the fold; who do not care for office, nor name, but for secret influence, and do all things occultly and cunningly, consenting to any servility of office or conduct, so only that they may intimately discern, and unawares direct, the minds of men. Then those who 'intrude' (thrust, that is) themselves into the fold, who by natural insolence of heart, and stout eloquence of tongue, and fearlessly perseverant self-assertion, obtain hearing and authority with the common crowd. Lastly, those who 'climb', who, by labour and learning, both stout and sound, but selfishly exerted in the cause of their own ambition, gain high dignities and authorities, and become 'lords over the heritage', though not 'ensamples to the flock'.

22. Now go on:–

Of other care they little reckoning make,
Than how to scramble at the shearers' feast.
Blind mouths–

I pause again, for this is a strange expression; a broken metaphor, one might think, careless and unscholarly.

Not so: its very audacity and pithiness are intended to make us look close at the phrase and remember it. Those two monosyllables express the precisely accurate contraries of right character, in the two great offices of the Church – those of bishop and pastor.

A 'Bishop' means 'a person who sees'.

26. Cf.: 'You are perhaps surprised to hear Horace spoken of as a pious person. You always feel as if he introduced the word 'Jupiter' only when he wanted a dactyl' (*Val d'Arno*, IX, 218 ff.). 'You think that all verses were written as an exercise, and that Minerva was only a convenient word for the last of a hexameter, and Jupiter for the last but one' (*The Queen of the Air*, I.47).

A 'Pastor' means 'a person who feeds'.

The most unbishoply character a man can have is therefore to be Blind.

The most unpastoral is, instead of feeding, to want to be fed,– to be a Mouth.

Take the two reverses together, and you have 'blind mouths'. We may advisably follow out this idea a little. Nearly all the evils in the Church have arisen from bishops desiring *power* more than *light*. They want authority, not outlook. Whereas their real office is not to rule; though it may be vigorously to exhort and rebuke: it is the king's office to rule; the bishop's office is to *oversee* the flock; to number it, sheep by sheep; to be ready always to give full account of it. Now it is clear he cannot give account of the souls, if he has not so much as numbered the bodies, of his flock. The first thing, therefore, that a bishop has to do is at least to put himself in a position in which, at any moment, he can obtain the history, from childhood, of every living soul in his diocese, and of its present state. Down in that back street, Bill and Nancy, knocking each other's teeth out!– Does the bishop know all about it? Has he his eye upon them? Has he *had* his eye upon them? Can he circumstantially explain to us how Bill got into the habit of beating Nancy about the head? If he cannot, he is no bishop, though he had a mitre as high as Salisbury steeple; he is no bishop,– he has sought to be at the helm instead of the masthead; he has no sight of things. 'Nay,' you say, 'it is not his duty to look after Bill in the back street'. What! the fat sheep that have full fleeces – you think it is only those he should look after while (go back to your Milton) 'the hungry sheep look up, and are not fed, besides what the grim wolf, with privy paw' (bishops knowing nothing about it), 'daily devours apace, and nothing said'?

'But that's not our idea of a bishop.'[27] Perhaps not; but it was St Paul's; and it was Milton's. They may be right, or we may be;

27. Compare the 13th Letter in *Time and Tide*. [Ruskin's note]

but we must not think we are reading either one or the other by putting our meaning into their words.

23. I go on.

But swoln with wind, and the rank mist they draw.

This is to meet the vulgar answer that 'if the poor are not looked after in their bodies, they are in their souls; they have spiritual food.'

And Milton says, 'They have no such thing as spiritual food; they are only swollen with wind.' At first you may think that is a coarse type, and an obscure one. But again, it is a quite literally accurate one. Take up your Latin and Greek dictionaries, and find out the meaning of 'Spirit'. It is only a contraction of the Latin word 'breath', and an indistinct translation of the Greek work for 'wind'. The same word is used in writing, 'The wind bloweth where it listeth'; and in writing, 'So is every one that is born of the Spirit';[28] born of the *breath*, that is; for it means the breath of God, in soul and body. We

---

28. John 3:8–9. I find further allusions to this passage in *On the Old Road*, III.274 and II.34: 'Then it cannot but occur to me to inquire how far this modern 'pneuma', Steam, may be connected with other pneumatic powers talked of in that old religious literature… what connection, I say, this modern 'spiritus', in its valve-directed inspiration, has with that more ancient spiritus, or warm breath, which people used to think they might be 'born of.' And in *The Queen of the Air*, III.55: 'What precise meaning we ought to attach to expressions such as that of the prophecy to the four winds that the dry bones might be breathed upon, and might live, or why the presence of the vital power should be dependent on the chemical action of the air… we cannot at present know… What we assuredly know is that the states of life and death are different, and the first more desirable than the other, and by effort attainable, whether we understand being 'born of the spirit' to signify having the breath of heaven in our flesh, or its power in our hearts.' – From another point of view, Ruskin is here, as just previously in *Sesame* and later, very often, in *The Bible of Amiens*, prohibiting us, with a transcendental 'this does not concern you', from asking questions of origin and of essence, and inviting us instead to concern ourselves with questions of moral and spiritual fact.

have the true sense of it in our words 'inspiration' and 'expire'. Now, there are two kinds of breath with which the flock may be filled,– God's breath, and man's. The breath of God is health, and life, and peace to them, as the air of heaven is to the flocks on the hills; but man's breath – the word which *he* calls spiritual – is disease and contagion to them, as the fog of the fen. They rot inwardly with it; they are puffed up by it, as a dead body by the vapours of its own decomposition. This is literally true of all false religious teaching; the first and last, and fatalest sign of it, is that 'puffing up'. Your converted children, who teach their parents; your converted convicts, who teach honest men; your converted dunces, who, having lived in cretinous stupefaction half their lives, suddenly awaking to the fact of there being a God, fancy themselves therefore His peculiar people and messengers; your sectarians of every species, small and great, Catholic or Protestant, of high church or low, in so far as they think themselves exclusively in the right and others wrong; and, pre-eminently, in every sect, those who hold that men can be saved by thinking rightly instead of doing rightly, by word instead of act, and wish instead of work;– these are the true fog children[29] – clouds, these, without water; bodies, these, of putrescent vapour and skin, without blood or flesh: blown bagpipes for

And behold, contemporary medicine too – though it partakes of a point of view so different, so alien, so opposed – is preparing to tell us that we are '*born of the spirit*', and that the spirit continues to control our respiration (see Dr Brugelmann's works on asthma), our digestion (Professor Dubois, University of Bern, *The Psychic Treatment of Nervous Disorders* and other works), and our muscular coordination (see *Isolation and Psychotherapy* by Dr Camus and Dr Pagniez, preface by Professor Déjerine). 'When you can dissect a dead body and show me its soul, I will believe in it', physicians liked to say twenty years ago; now, it is not in dead bodies (which, in the wise theory of Ezekiel, are dead bodies precisely because they no longer have a soul [Ezek. 37:1–12]), but in the living body – at every step, in every disordered function – that they sense the presence and action of the soul, and to cure the body it is the soul that they address themselves to. Doctors said not long ago

the fiends to pipe with – corrupt, and corrupting,– 'Swollen with wind, and the rank mist they draw'.

24. Lastly, let us return to the lines respecting the power of the keys, for now we can understand them. Note the difference between Milton and Dante in their interpretation of this power: for once, the latter is weaker in thought; he supposes *both* the keys to be of the gate of heaven; one is of gold, the other of silver: they are given by St Peter to the sentinel angel; and it is not easy to determine the meaning either of the substances of the three steps of the gate, or of the two keys. But Milton makes one, of gold, the key of heaven; the other, of iron, the key of the prison in which the wicked teachers are to be bound who 'have taken away the key of knowledge, yet entered not in themselves.'

We have seen that the duties of bishop and pastor are to see, and feed; and of all who do so it is said, 'He that watereth, shall be watered also himself.' But the reverse is truth also. He that watereth not, shall be *withered* himself; and he that seeth not, shall himself be shut out of sight – shut into the perpetual prison-house. And that prison opens here, as well as hereafter: he who is to be bound in heaven must first be bound on earth. That command to the strong angels, of which the rock-apostle is the image, 'Take him, and bind him hand and foot, and cast him

---

(and hack writers belatedly repeat it even now) that a pessimist is a man with a bad stomach. Today, Dr Dubois states in black and white that a man with a bad stomach is a pessimist, and it is no longer his stomach that has to be cured if we want to change his philosophy, it is his philosophy that has to be changed if we want to cure his stomach. We are of course leaving aside here the metaphysical questions of origin and essence. Absolute materialism and pure idealism are equally obliged to distinguish between body and soul: for idealism the body is a lesser spirit, something still of the spirit but darkened; for materialism the soul is still matter but more complex, more subtle. The distinction between body and soul persists, in both cases, for reasons of linguistic convenience, even if both philosophies are forced to equate their natures in order to explain their reciprocal action upon each other.

29. Cf. *Bible of Amiens* III, 41.

out',[30] issues, in its measure, against the teacher, for every help withheld, and for every truth refused, and for every falsehood enforced; so that he is more strictly fettered the more he fetters, and farther outcast as he more and more misleads, till at last the bars of the iron cage close upon him, and as 'the golden opes, the iron shuts amain'.

25. We have got something out of the lines, I think, and much more is yet to be found in them; but we have done enough by way of example of the kind of word-by-word examination of your author which is rightly called 'reading'; watching every accent and expression, and putting ourselves always in the author's place, annihilating our own personality, and seeking to enter into his, so as to be able assuredly to say, 'Thus Milton thought', not 'Thus *I* thought, in mis-reading Milton.' And by this process you will gradually come to attach less weight to your own 'Thus I thought' at other times. You will begin to perceive that what *you* thought was a matter of no serious importance;– that your thoughts on any subject are not perhaps the clearest and wisest that could be arrived at thereupon:– in fact, that unless you are a very singular person, you cannot be said to have any 'thoughts' at all; that you have no materials for them, in any serious matters;[31]–no right to 'think', but only to try to learn more of the facts. Nay, most probably all your life (unless, as I said, you are a singular person) you will have no legitimate right to an 'opinion'

30. An allusion to the verses in Matthew which will forever remain the most amusing portrait there is of an excessively rigid master of the house, about whom his guests say, with reason: He is terrible. The passage is as follows: 'And when the king came in to see the guests, he saw there a man which had not on a wedding garment: And he saith unto him, Friend, how camest thou in hither not having a wedding garment? And he was speechless. Then said the king to the servants, Bind him hand and foot, and take him away, and cast him into outer darkness, there shall be weeping and gnashing of teeth. For many are called, but few are chosen.' (Matt. 22:12–14)
31. Modern 'Education' for the most part signifies giving people the faculty of thinking wrong on every conceivable subject of importance to them. [Ruskin's note]

on any business, except that instantly under your hand. What must of necessity be done, you can always find out, beyond question, how to do. Have you a house to keep in order, a commodity to sell, a field to plough, a ditch to cleanse? There need be no two opinions about these proceedings; it is at your peril if you have not much more than an 'opinion' on the way to manage such matters. And also, outside of your own business, there are one or two subjects on which you are bound to have but one opinion. That roguery and lying are objectionable, and are instantly to be flogged out of the way whenever discovered;– that covetousness and love of quarrelling are dangerous dispositions even in children, and deadly dispositions in men and nations;– that, in the end, the God of heaven and earth loves active, modest, and kind people, and hates idle, proud, greedy, and cruel ones;– on these general facts you are bound to have but one, and that a very strong, opinion. For the rest, respecting religions, governments, sciences, arts, you will find that, on the whole, you can know NOTHING,– judge nothing; that the best you can do, even though you may be a well-educated person, is to be silent, and strive to be wiser every day, and to understand a little more of the thoughts of others, which so soon as you try to do honestly, you will discover that the thoughts even of the wisest are very little more than pertinent questions. To put the difficulty into a clear shape, and exhibit to you the grounds for *in*decision, that is all they can generally do for you!– and well for them and for us, if indeed they are able 'to mix the music with our thoughts and sadden us with heavenly doubts'.[32] This writer, from whom I have been reading to you, is not among the first or wisest: he sees shrewdly as far as he sees, and therefore it is easy to find out its full meaning; but with the greater men, you cannot fathom their meaning; they do not even wholly measure it themselves,– it is so wide. Suppose I had asked you, for instance, to seek for Shakespeare's opinion, instead of Milton's

32. The Library Edition gives the reference: Emerson, 'To Rhea'.

on this matter of Church authority?– or for Dante's? Have any of you, at this instant, the least idea what either thought about it? Have you ever balanced the scene with the bishops in *Richard III* against the character of Cranmer?[33] the description of St Francis and St Dominic against that of him who made Virgil wonder to gaze upon him,– 'disteso, tanto vilmente, nell' eterno esilio': or of him whom Dante stood beside, 'come 'I frate che confessa lo perfido assassin?'[34] Shakespeare and Alighieri knew men better than most of us, I presume! They were both in the midst of the main struggle between the temporal and spiritual powers. They had an opinion, we may guess. But where is it? Bring it into court! Put Shakespeare's or Dante's creed into articles, and send *it* up for trial by the Ecclesiastical Courts!

26. You will not be able, I tell you again, for many and many a day, to come at the real purposes and teaching of these great men; but a very little honest study of them will enable you to perceive that what you took for your own 'judgment' was mere chance prejudice, and drifted, helpless, entangled weed of cast-away thought; nay, you will see that most men's minds are indeed little better than rough heath wilderness, neglected and stubborn, partly barren, partly overgrown with pestilent brakes, and venomous, wind-sown herbage of evil surmise; that the first thing you have to do for them, and yourself, is eagerly and scornfully to set fire to *this;* burn all the jungle into wholesome ash-heaps, and then plough and sow. All the true literary work before you, for life, must begin with obedience to that order, 'Break up your fallow ground, and *sow not among thorns.*'

27. (II.[35]) Having then faithfully listened to the great teachers, that you may enter into their Thoughts, you have yet this higher advance to make;—you have to enter into their Hearts. As you go to them first for clear sight, so you must stay

33. In *Henry VIII.*
34. *Inf.* xxiii. 125, 126; xix. 49, 50. [Ruskin's note]
35. Compare § 13 above. [Ruskin's note]

with them, that you may share at last their just and mighty Passion. Passion, or 'sensation'. I am not afraid of the word; still less of the thing. You have heard many outcries against sensation lately; but, I can tell you, it is not less sensation we want, but more. The ennobling difference between one man and another,– between one animal and another,– is precisely in this, that one feels more than another. If we were sponges, perhaps sensation might not be easily got for us; if we were earth-worms, liable at every instant to be cut in two by the spade, perhaps too much sensation might not be good for us. But being human creatures, it *is* good for us; nay, we are only human in so far as we are sensitive, and our honour is precisely in proportion to our passion.[36]

28. You know I said of that great and pure society of the Dead, that it would allow 'no vain or vulgar person to enter there'. What do you think I meant by a 'vulgar' person? What do you yourselves mean by 'vulgarity'? You will find it a fruitful subject of thought; but, briefly, the essence of all vulgarity lies in want of sensation. Simple and innocent vulgarity is merely an untrained and undeveloped bluntness of body and mind; but in true inbred vulgarity, there is a dreadful callousness, which, in extremity, becomes capable of every sort of bestial habit and crime, without fear, without pleasure, without horror, and without pity.[37] It is in the blunt hand and the dead heart, in the diseased habit, in the hardened conscience, that men become vulgar; they are for ever vulgar, precisely in proportion as they are incapable of sympathy,– of quick understanding,– of all

36. Cf. Anatole France's worthy *My Friend's Book:* 'There!' I cried; 'there we have a manifestation of the passions. But let us not speak ill of the passions; they are the mainspring of all the great deeds that are wrought in this world. My daughter… let your passions be strong, let them wax greater, and yourself grow stronger with them. And if in after years you become their inexorable mistress, their strength will be your strength, and their loftiness your beauty. The passions make up the whole of man's moral riches.'
37. Cf. *The Bible of Amiens:* 'one artless, letterless, and merciless monastery'.

that, in deep insistence on the common, but most accurate term, may be called the 'tact' or 'touch-faculty', of body and soul: that tact which the Mimosa has in trees, which the pure woman has above all creatures; fineness and fulness of sensation, beyond reason;– the guide and sanctifier of reason itself. Reason can but determine what is true:– it is the God-given passion of humanity which alone can recognise what God has made good.

29. We come then to that great concourse of the Dead, not merely to know from them what is True, but chiefly to feel with them what is just. Now, to feel with them, we must be like them; and none of us can become that without pains. As the true knowledge is disciplined and tested knowledge,– not the first thought that comes, so the true passion is disciplined and tested passion,– not the first passion that comes. The first that come are the vain, the false, the treacherous; if you yield to them they will lead you wildly and far, in vain pursuit, in hollow enthusiasm, till you have no true purpose and no true passion left. Not that any feeling possible to humanity is in itself wrong, but only wrong when undisciplined. Its nobility is in its force and justice; it is wrong when it is weak, and felt for paltry cause. There is a mean wonder, as of a child who sees a juggler tossing golden balls; and this is base, if you will. But do you think that the wonder is ignoble, or the sensation less, with which every human soul is called to watch the golden balls of heaven tossed through the night by the Hand that made them? There is a mean curiosity, as of a child opening a forbidden door, or a servant prying into her master's business;– and a noble curiosity, questioning, in the front of danger, the source of the great river beyond the sand,– the place of the great continents beyond the sea;– a nobler curiosity still, which questions of the source of the River of Life, and of the space of the Continent of Heaven,– things which 'the angels desire to look into'. So the anxiety is ignoble, with which you linger over the course and catastrophe of an idle tale; but do you think the

anxiety is less, or greater, with which you watch, or *ought* to watch, the dealings of fate and destiny with the life of an agonised nation? Alas! it is the narrowness, selfishness, minuteness, of your sensation that you have to deplore in England at this day;– sensation which spends itself in bouquets and speeches: in revellings and junketings; in sham fights and gay puppet shows, while you can look on and see noble nations murdered, man by man, without an effort or a tear.[38]

30. I said 'minuteness' and 'selfishness' of sensation, but it would have been enough to have said 'injustice' or 'unrighteousness' of sensation. For as in nothing is a gentleman better to be discerned from a vulgar person, so in nothing is a gentle nation (such nations have been) better to be discerned from a mob, than in this,– that their feelings are constant and just, results of due contemplation, and of equal thought. You can talk a mob into anything; its feelings may be – usually are – on the whole, generous and right; but it has no foundation for them, no hold of them; you may tease or tickle it into any, at your pleasure; it thinks by infection, for the most part, catching an opinion like a cold, and there is nothing so little that it will not roar itself wild about, when the fit is on;– nothing so great but it will forget in an hour, when the fit is past. But a gentleman's, or a gentle nation's, passions are just, measured, and continuous. A great nation, for instance, does not spend its entire national wits for a couple of months in weighing evidence of a single ruffian's having done a single murder;[39] and for a couple of years see its own children murder each other by their thousands or tens of thousands a day, considering only what the effect is likely to be on the price

38. An allusion to the destruction of Poland (1864).

39. The Library Edition informs us that this is an allusion to the heightened public interest that year in the murder of a man named Briggs on the North London line (attested in the newspapers of October and November, 1864). Matthew Arnold comments ironically on the demoralisation of our class as a result of the Bow tragedy in his 1865 preface to the *Essay on Criticism.*

of cotton, and caring no wise to determine which side of battle is in the wrong.[40] Neither does a great nation send its poor little boys to jail for stealing six walnuts; and allow its bankrupts to steal their hundreds of thousands with a bow, and its bankers, rich with poor men's savings, to close their doors 'under circumstances over which they have no control', with a 'by your leave'; and large landed estates to be bought by men who have made their money by going with armed steamers up and down the China Seas, selling opium at the cannon's mouth,[41] and altering, for the benefit of the foreign nation, the common highwayman's demand of 'your money *or* your life', into that of 'your money *and* your life'. Neither does a great nation allow the lives of its innocent poor to be parched out of them by fog fever, and rotted out of them by dunghill plague, for the sake of sixpence a life extra per week to its landlords;[42] and then debate, with drivelling tears, and diabolical sympathies, whether it ought not piously to save, and nursingly cherish, the lives of its murderers. Also, a great nation having made up its mind that hanging is quite the wholesomest process for its homicides in general, can yet with mercy distinguish between the degrees of guilt in homicides; and does not yelp[43] like a pack of frost-pinched wolf-cubs on the blood-track of an unhappy crazed boy, or grey-haired clodpate Othello, 'perplexed i' the extreme', at the very moment that it is sending a Minister of the Crown[44] to make polite speeches to a man who is bayoneting young girls in their fathers' sight,

---

40. An allusion, according to the Library Edition, to the American Civil War and the interruption of the cotton trade due to the blockade of the Southern ports.

41. An allusion, the same edition says, to the wars of 1840 and 1856 caused by Chinese resistance to the opium trade.

42. See note at end of lecture. [Ruskin's note. The note he cross-references is omitted in this edition – D.S.]

43. Unfortunately, the Library Edition does not supply the contemporary fact to which Ruskin is alluding.

and killing noble youths in cool blood, faster than a country butcher kills lambs in spring. And, lastly, a great nation does not mock Heaven and its Powers, by pretending belief in a revelation which asserts the love of money to be the root of *all* evil, and declaring, at the same time, that it is actuated, and intends to be actuated, in all chief national deeds and measures, by no other love.

31. My friends, I do not know why any of us should talk about reading. We want some sharper discipline than that of reading; but, at all events, be assured, we cannot read. No reading is possible for a people with its mind in this state. No sentence of any great writer is intelligible to them. It is simply and sternly impossible for the English public, at this moment, to understand any thoughtful writing,– so incapable of thought has it become in its insanity of avarice. Happily, our disease is, as yet, little worse than this incapacity of thought; it is not corruption of the inner nature; we ring true still, when anything strikes home to us; and though the idea that everything should 'pay' has infected our every purpose so deeply, that even when we would play the good Samaritan,[45] we never take out our two pence and give them to the host, without saying, 'When I come again, thou shalt give me fourpence', there is a capacity of noble passion left in our hearts' core. We show it in our work – in our war,– even in those unjust domestic affections which make us furious at a small private wrong, while we are polite to a boundless public one: we are still industrious to the last hour of the day, though we add the gambler's fury to the labourer's patience; we are still brave to the death, though incapable of discerning true cause for battle; and are still true in affection to our own flesh, to the death, as the sea-monsters are, and the rock-eagles. And there is

44. The new ambassador whom England had just sent to Russia in the same year as the massacres in Poland, which was also the year that this lecture was given. The Library Edition supplies this ambassador's name: Sir Andrew Buchanan.
45. Cf. Luke 10:30 ff.

hope for a nation while this can be still said of it. As long as it holds its life in its hand, ready to give it for its honour (though a foolish honour), for its love (though a selfish love), and for its business (though a base business), there is hope for it. But hope only; for this instinctive, reckless virtue cannot last. No nation can last, which has made a mob of itself, however generous at heart. It must discipline its passions, and direct them, or they will discipline *it*, one day, with scorpion whips.[46] Above all, a nation cannot last as a money-making mob: it cannot with impunity,– it cannot with existence,– go on despising literature, despising science, despising art, despising nature, despising compassion, and concentrating its soul on Pence. Do you think these are harsh or wild words? Have patience with me but a little longer. I will prove their truth to you, clause by clause.

32. (I.) I say first we have despised literature. What do we, as a nation, care about books? How much do you think we spend altogether on our libraries, public or private, as compared with what we spend on our horses?[47] If a man spends lavishly on his library, you call him mad – a bibliomaniac. But you never call any one a horsemaniac, though men ruin themselves every day by their horses, and you do not hear of people ruining themselves by their books. Or, to go lower still, how much do you think the contents of the book-shelves of the United Kingdom, public and private, would fetch, as compared with the contents of its wine-cellars? What position would its expenditure on literature take, as compared with its expenditure on luxurious eating? We talk of food for the mind, as of food for the body: now a good book contains such food inexhaustibly; it is a provision for life, and for the best part of us; yet how long most people would look at the best book before they would give

46. Probably a vague allusion to Kings 12:14: the speech which Rehoboam gives, forsaking the old men's counsel but following the counsel of the young men, 'saying, My father chastised you with whips, but I will chastise you with scorpions [i.e., pointed whips].'
47. Cf. *Munera Pulveris* 65. [Ruskin's note]

the price of a large turbot for it? Though there have been men who have pinched their stomachs and bared their backs to buy a book, whose libraries were cheaper to them, I think, in the end, than most men's dinners are. We are few of us put to such trial, and more the pity; for, indeed, a precious thing is all the more precious to us if it has been won by work or economy; and if public libraries were half so costly as public dinners, or books cost the tenth part of what bracelets do, even foolish men and women might sometimes suspect there was good in reading, as well as in munching and sparkling: whereas the very cheapness of literature is making even wise people forget that if a book is worth reading, it is worth buying. No book is worth anything which is not worth *much*; nor is it serviceable, until it has been read, and re-read, and loved, and loved again; and marked, so that you can refer to the passages you want in it, as a soldier can seize the weapon he needs in an armoury, or a housewife bring the spice she needs from her store. Bread of flour is good; but there is bread, sweet as honey, if we would eat it, in a good book; and the family must be poor indeed, which, once in their lives, cannot, for such multipliable barley-loaves, pay their baker's bill. We call ourselves a rich nation, and we are filthy and foolish enough to thumb each other's books out of circulating libraries!

33. (II.) I say we have despised science. [...]

34. (III.) I say you have despised Art! [...]

35. (IV.) You have despised Nature; that is to say, all the deep and sacred sensations of natural scenery. The French revolutionists made stables of the cathedrals of France; you have made race-courses of the cathedrals of the earth. Your *one* conception of pleasure is to drive in railroad carriages round their aisles, and eat off their altars.[48] [...]You have put

48. I meant that the beautiful places of the world – Switzerland, Italy, South Germany, and so on – are, indeed, the truest cathedrals – places to be reverent in, and to worship in; and that we only care to drive through them: and to eat and drink at their most sacred places. [Ruskin's note]

a railroad-bridge over the falls of Schaffhausen. You have tunnelled the cliffs of Lucerne by Tell's chapel; you have destroyed the Clarens shore of the Lake of Geneva; there is not a quiet valley in England that you have not filled with bellowing fire; there is no particle left of English land which you have not trampled coal ashes into[49] – nor any foreign city in which the spread of your presence is not marked among its fair old streets and happy gardens by a consuming white leprosy of new hotels and perfumers' shops: the Alps themselves,[50] which your own poets used to love so reverently, you look upon as soaped poles in a bear-garden, which you set yourselves to climb and slide down again, with 'shrieks of delight'. When you are past shrieking, having no human articulate voice to say you are glad with, you fill the quietude of their valleys with gunpowder blasts, and rush home, red with

49. I was singularly struck, some years ago, by finding all the river shore at Richmond, in Yorkshire, black in its earth, from the mere drift of soot-laden air from places many miles away. [Ruskin's note]

50. Compare this to the end of the Preface of *The Queen of the Air*: 'This first day of May, 1869, I am writing where my work was begun thirty-five years ago, within sight of the snows of the higher Alps. In that half of the permitted life of man, I have seen strange evil brought upon every scene that I best loved, or tried to make beloved by others. The light... the air... the waters... are dimmed and foul. This morning, on the Lake of Geneva, at half a mile from the beach, I could scarcely see my oar-blade a fathom deep. By the last marble of the foot of Jura, sloping to the blue water, and (at this time of year) covered with bright pink tufts of Saponaria, was a newly-constructed artificial rockery, with an inscription on one of its loose-tumbled stones,–

Aux Botanistes,
Le club Jurassique,

Ah, masters of modern science, give me back my Athena out of your vials, and seal, if it may be, once more, Asmodeus therein. Teach us, now, but this, which is all that man need know,– that the Air is given to him for his life; and the Rain to his thirst, and for his baptism; and the Fire for warmth; and the Sun for sight; and the Earth for his meat—and his Rest.' I have

cutaneous eruption of conceit, and voluble with convulsive hiccough of self-satisfaction. I think nearly the two sorrow-fullest spectacles I have ever seen in humanity, taking the deep inner significance of them, are the English mobs in the valley of Chamouni, amusing themselves with firing rusty howitzers; and the Swiss vintagers of Zurich expressing their Christian thanks for the gift of the vine, by assembling in knots in the 'towers of the vineyards',[51] and slowly loading and firing horse-pistols from morning till evening.[52] It is pitiful, to have dim conceptions of duty; more pitiful, it seems to me, to have conceptions like these, of mirth.

36. Lastly. You despise compassion. There is no need of words of mine for proof of this. I will merely print one of the newspaper paragraphs which I am in the habit of cutting out and throwing into my store-drawer [....] I will print the

abbreviated this passage following La Sizeranne, but note that he gives '*repos*' with a lowercase *r* for 'Rest'; I prefer '*Repos*', restoring the capital letter as it appears in Ruskin's text. We can understand from its sudden grandeur the kind of rest in question. Admittedly, one could argue that Ruskin is not referring here to the rest of the tomb, and one could support this assertion with a passage from the Preface to *The Crown of Wild Olive*: 'was this grass of the earth made green for your shroud only, not for your bed? and can you never lie down *upon* it, but only *under* it?' Despite this uncertainty, which I acknowledge, I nevertheless believe, above all because of the capital letter and the importance given to the last word of the Preface, that the rest in question here is that of the tomb.

51. Ruskin alludes here to the passage in Matthew (21:33 ff.; or the same passage in Isaiah 5:2): 'There was a certain householder, which planted a vineyard, and hedged it round about, and digged a winepress in it, and built a tower' (to be able to survey the vineyard). He had already alluded to these verses in *Lectures of Architecture and Painting*, §19, when, listing all the passages in the Bible that mention towers, he says: 'you recollect the husbandman building a tower in his vineyard.' Ruskin means to demonstrate (with respect to the religious value of Gothic architecture) that towers are never religious in nature in the Bible; they are built only out of pride, for pleasure, or for defense.

52. Cf. *Time and Tide*, §46.

paragraph in red.[53] Be sure, the facts themselves are written in that colour, in a book which we shall all of us, literate or illiterate, have to read our page of, some day.[54] [...]

39. When men are rightly occupied, their amusement grows out of their work, as the colour-petals out of a fruitful flower;– when they are faithfully helpful and compassionate, all their emotions become steady, deep, perpetual, and vivifying to the soul as the natural pulse to the body. But now, having no true business, we pour our whole masculine energy into the false business of money-making; and having no true emotion, we must have false emotions dressed up for us to play with, not innocently, as children with dolls, but guiltily and darkly, as the idolatrous Jews with their pictures on cavern walls, which men had to dig to detect.[55] The justice we do not execute, we mimic in the novel and on the stage; for the beauty we destroy in nature, we substitute the metamorphosis of the pantomime, and (the human nature of us imperatively requiring awe and sorrow of *some* kind) for the noble grief we should have borne with our fellows, and the pure tears we should have wept with them, we gloat over the pathos of the police court, and gather the night-dew of the grave.

---

53. The entire paragraph is in fact printed in red in the English text. We had wanted to do the same in the French, to preserve the strange effect of these pages in the original, but practical difficulties prevented it.

54. Cf. *Stones of Venice*: 'a message that once was written in blood and a sound that one day shall fill the vault of heaven' (I.IV.71); and *Crown of Wild Olive*, II.59: 'when the whole world turns clown, and paints itself red with its own heart's blood instead of vermilion'.

55. An allusion to this strange passage in Ezekiel: 'Then said he unto me: Son of man, dig now in the wall; and when I had digged in the wall, behold a door... So I went in and saw; and behold every form of creeping things, and abominable beasts, and all the idols of the house of Israel, portrayed upon the wall round about. And there stood before them seventy men... with every man his censer in his hand; and a thick cloud of incense went up. Then said he unto me: Son of man, hast thou seen what the ancients of the house of Israel do in the dark, every man in the chambers of his imagery?' (Ezek. 8:6–18).

40. It is difficult to estimate the true significance of these things; the facts are frightful enough;– the measure of national fault involved in them is perhaps not as great as it would at first seem. We permit, or cause, thousands of deaths daily, but we mean no harm; we set fire to houses, and ravage peasants' fields, yet we should be sorry to find we had injured anybody. We are still kind at heart; still capable of virtue, but only as children are. Chalmers, at the end of his long life, having had much power with the public, being plagued in some serious matter by a reference to 'public opinion', uttered the impatient exclamation, 'The public is just a great baby!' And the reason that I have allowed all these graver subjects of thought to mix themselves up with an inquiry into methods of reading, is that, the more I see of our national faults or miseries, the more they resolve themselves into conditions of childish illiterateness and want of education in the most ordinary habits of thought. It is, I repeat, not vice, not selfishness, not dullness of brain, which we have to lament; but an unreachable schoolboy's recklessness, only differing from the true schoolboy's in its incapacity of being helped, because it acknowledges no master.

41. There is a curious type of us given in one of the lovely, neglected works of the last of our great painters.[56] It is a drawing of Kirkby Lonsdale churchyard, and of its brook, and valley, and hills, and folded morning sky beyond. And unmindful alike of these, and of the dead who have left these for other valleys and for other skies, a group of schoolboys have piled their little books upon a grave, to strike them off with stones. So, also, we play with the words of the dead that would teach us, and strike them far from us with our bitter, reckless will; little thinking that those leaves which the wind scatters had been piled, not only upon a gravestone, but upon the seal of an enchanted vault – nay, the gate of a great city of sleeping kings, who would

56. Turner. On this drawing, its pathos, and its meaning, see *Modern Painters*, V.I.17 and V.XVIII.2.

awake for us and walk with us, if we knew but how to call them by their names. How often, even if we lift the marble entrance gate, do we but wander among those old kings in their repose, and finger the robes they lie in, and stir the crowns on their foreheads; and still they are silent to us, and seem but a dusty imagery; because we know not the incantation of the heart that would wake them;– which, if they once heard, they would start up to meet us in their power of long ago, narrowly to look upon us, and consider us; and, as the fallen kings of Hades meet the newly fallen, saying, 'Art thou also become weak as we – art thou also become one of us?' so would these kings, with their undimmed, unshaken diadems, meet us, saying, 'Art thou also become pure and mighty of heart as we – art thou also become one of us?'

42. Mighty of heart, mighty of mind – 'magnanimous' – to be this, is indeed to be great in life; to become this increasingly, is, indeed, to 'advance in life',– in life itself – not in the trappings of it. My friends, do you remember that old Scythian custom, when the head of a house died? How he was dressed in his finest dress, and set in his chariot, and carried about to his friends' houses; and each of them placed him at his table's head, and all feasted in his presence? Suppose it were offered to you in plain words, as it *is* offered to you in dire facts, that you should gain this Scythian honour, gradually, while you yet thought yourself alive. Suppose the offer were this: You shall die slowly; your blood shall daily grow cold, your flesh petrify, your heart beat at last only as a rusted group of iron valves.[57] Your life shall fade from you, and sink through the earth into the ice of Caina;[58] but, day by day, your body shall be dressed more gaily, and set

57. The physical analogy is the offer of arteriosclerosis which the demon of good living makes every day to arthritics. But here too, with health as with genius, temperament is stronger than the doctor's orders.
58. The circle of Hell in Dante which bears the name of Cain. See *Inferno*, cantos V and XXXII.

in higher chariots, and have more orders on its breast – crowns on its head, if you will. Men shall bow before it, stare and shout round it, crowd after it up and down the streets; build palaces for it, feast with it at their tables' heads all the night long; your soul shall stay enough within it to know what they do, and feel the weight of the golden dress on its shoulders, and the furrow of the crown-edge on the skull;– no more. Would you take the offer, verbally made by the death-angel? Would the meanest among us take it, think you? Yet practically and verily we grasp at it, every one of us, in a measure; many of us grasp at it in its fulness of horror. Every man accepts it, who desires to advance in life without knowing what life is; who means only that he is to get more horses, and more footmen, and more fortune, and more public honour, and – *not* more personal soul. He only is advancing in life, whose heart is getting softer, whose blood warmer, whose brain quicker, whose spirit is entering into Living[59] peace. And the men who have this life in them are the true lords or kings of the earth – they, and they only. All other kingships, so far as they are true, are only the practical issue and expression of theirs; if less than this, they are either dramatic royalties,– costly shows, set off, indeed, with real jewels, instead of tinsel – but still only the toys of nations; or else they are no royalties at all, but tyrannies, or the mere active and practical issue of national folly; for which reason I have said of them elsewhere, 'Visible governments are the toys of some nations, the diseases of others, the harness of some, the burdens of more.'

43. But I have no words for the wonder with which I hear Kinghood still spoken of, even among thoughtful men, as if governed nations were a personal property, and might be bought and sold, or otherwise acquired, as sheep, of whose flesh their king was to feed, and whose fleece he was to gather; as if

59. 'τὸ δὲ φρόνημα τοῦ πνεύματος ζωὴ καὶ εἰρήνη' [Ruskin's note]
(Romans 8:6: 'To be spiritually minded is life and peace'.)

Achilles' indignant epithet of base kings, 'people-eating', were the constant and proper title of all monarchs; and the enlargement of a king's dominion meant the same thing as the increase of a private man's estate! Kings who think so, however powerful, can no more be the true kings of the nation than gadflies are the kings of a horse; they suck it, and may drive it wild, but do not guide it. They, and their courts, and their armies are, if one could see clearly, only a large species of marsh mosquito, with bayonet proboscis and melodious, band-mastered trumpeting, in the summer air; the twilight being, perhaps, sometimes fairer, but hardly more wholesome, for its glittering mists of midge companies. The true kings, meanwhile, rule quietly, if at all, and hate ruling; too many of them make 'il gran rifiuto';[60] and if they do not, the mob, as soon as they are likely to become useful to it, is pretty sure to make *its* 'gran rifiuto' of *them*.

44. Yet the visible king may also be a true one, some day, if ever day comes when he will estimate his dominion by the *force* of it,– not the geographical boundaries. It matters very little whether Trent cuts you a cantel out here, or Rhine rounds you a castle less there.[61] But it does matter to you, king of men, whether you can verily say to this man, 'Go', and he goeth; and to another, 'Come', and he cometh. Whether you can turn your people, as you can Trent – and where it is that you bid them come, and where go.[62] It matters to you, king of men, whether your people hate you, and die by you, or love you, and live by you. You may measure your dominion by multitudes, better than by miles; and count degrees of love-latitude, not from, but to, a wonderfully warm and infinite equator.[63]

60. An allusion to Dante, *Inferno* III, 60.
61. An allusion to Shakespeare's *Henry IV, Part I*, Act 3, Scene 1.
62. It is the centurion of Capernaum who says to Jesus: 'I have soldiers under me: and I say to this man, Go, and he goeth; and to another, Come, and he cometh; and to my servant, Do this, and he doeth it' (Matt. 8:9).

45. Measure! – nay, you cannot measure. Who shall measure the difference between the power of those who 'do and teach',[64] and who are greatest in the kingdoms of earth, as of heaven – and the power of those who undo, and consume – whose power, at the fullest, is only the power of the moth and the rust? Strange! to think how the Moth-kings lay up treasures for the moth; and the Rust-kings, who are to their peoples' strength as rust to armour, lay up treasures for the rust; and the Robber-kings, treasures for the robber; but how few kings have ever laid up treasures that needed no guarding – treasures of which, the more thieves there were, the better! Broidered robe, only to be rent; helm and sword, only to be dimmed; jewel and gold, only to be scattered;– there have been three kinds of kings who have gathered these. Suppose there ever should arise a Fourth order of kings, who had read, in some obscure writing of long ago, that there was a Fourth kind of treasure, which the jewel and gold could not equal, neither should it be valued with pure gold. A web made fair in the weaving, by Athena's shuttle; an armour, forged in divine fire by Vulcanian force; a gold to be mined in the very sun's red heart, where he sets over the Delphian cliffs;– deep-pictured tissue;– impenetrable armour;– potable gold!–[65] the three

63. Cf.: 'Man is the sun of the world; more than the real sun. The fire of his wonderful heart is the only light and heat worth gauge or measure. Where he is, are the tropics; where he is not, the ice-world' (*Modern Painters* V, p. 225, quoted by Bardoux in his book on Ruskin).
64. If there were only this phrase 'do and teach', the most direct reference would seem to be to Acts 1:1 ('all that Jesus began both to do and teach'), but the context suggests that the reference is rather to Matthew 5:19: 'Whosoever therefore shall break one of these least commandments, and shall teach men so, he shall be called the least in the kingdom of heaven: but whosoever shall do and teach them, the same shall be called great in the kingdom of heaven' – and, Ruskin adds, in the kingdoms of earth.
65. The Library Edition informs us that this is the term used in alchemy for gold dissolved in nitro-hydrochloric acid, supposed to contain the elixir of life.

great Angels[66] of Conduct, Toil, and Thought, still calling to us, and waiting at the posts of our doors, to lead us, with their winged power, and guide us, with their unerring eyes, by the path which no fowl knoweth, and which the vulture's eye has not seen![67] Suppose kings should ever arise, who heard and believed this word, and at last gathered and brought forth treasures of – Wisdom – for their people?

46. Think what an amazing business *that* would be! How inconceivable, in the state of our present national wisdom! That we should bring up our peasants to a book exercise instead of a bayonet exercise!– organise, drill, maintain with pay, and good generalship, armies of thinkers, instead of armies of stabbers!– find national amusement in reading-rooms as well as rifle-grounds; give prizes for a fair shot at a fact, as well as for a leaden splash on a target. What an absurd idea it seems, put fairly in words, that the wealth of the capitalists of civilised nations should ever come to support literature instead of war!

[...]

49. I hope it will not be long before royal or national libraries will be founded in every considerable city, with a royal series of books in them; the same series in every one of them, chosen books, the best in every kind, prepared for that national series in the most perfect way possible; their text printed all on leaves of equal size, broad of margin, and divided into pleasant volumes, light in the hand, beautiful, and strong, and thorough as examples of binders' work; and that these great libraries will be accessible to all clean and orderly persons at all times of the day and evening; strict law being enforced for this cleanliness and quietness.

50. I could shape for you other plans, for art galleries, and for natural history galleries, and for many precious – many, it seems to me, needful – things; but this book plan is the easiest

66. Minerva, Vulcan, Apollo (see *On the Old Road*, II.36).
67. Job 28:7.

and needfullest, and would prove a considerable tonic to what we call our British constitution, which has fallen dropsical of late, and has an evil thirst, and evil hunger, and wants healthier feeding. You have got its corn laws repealed for it; try if you cannot get corn laws established for it, dealing in a better bread;– bread made of that old enchanted Arabian grain, the Sesame, which opens doors;– doors not of robbers', but of Kings', Treasuries.[68]

68. See footnote 1 above on this final sentence for an analysis of the five 'themes' it blends together (and, without descending into excessive subtlety, it is easy to arrive at seven themes, if we include the 'corn laws' and the 'better bread').

Makeshift Memory

I have here translated *The Bible of Amiens*, by John Ruskin, but this does not seem to be enough for the reader, in my view. To read only one book by an author is to see him only once. You can distinguish someone's individual traits in a single conversation, but it is only through repeated encounters in different circumstances that you can recognise these traits as characteristic and essential, and for a writer, for a musician or a painter, the varying circumstances that allow you, by a sort of controlled experiment, to discern the permanent aspects of his character are his various works. We find again, in a second book, in another painting, the particularities which, the first time, we might have believed depended on the subject matter. Putting the different works side by side brings out the common elements whose interrelation constitutes the moral physiognomy of the artist. When multiple Rembrandt portraits painted from different models are reunited in a gallery, we are struck at once by what is common to them all, the very features of the Rembrandt face. So, by adding a footnote every time a passage of *The Bible of Amiens* awakened in me, by analogies and correspondences however remote, the memory of other works of Ruskin's, and by translating in the footnote whatever text came, or returned, to mind, I have tried to enable the reader to put himself in the position of someone who has been in Ruskin's presence before, someone who, having conversed with him already, can recognise in his words that which is permanent and fundamental to Ruskin himself. I have tried in this way to provide for the reader a kind of makeshift memory, in which I have stored away recollections of Ruskin's other books – a sort of echo chamber where the words of *The Bible of Amiens* can resonate more deeply by awakening the echoes of their brothers. But doubtless these echoes will not, as they would in a memory which had formed on its own, answer the words of *The Bible of Amiens* from the horizons that are generally hidden from our sight, horizons at various distances which our life itself, day by day, measures out. The echoes will not rejoin this word, whose similarity has drawn them to it, by crossing the gentle resistance of that intervening atmosphere which has the dimensions of our life itself and which is the entire poetry of memory.

The fact is, the primary task of every critic should be to help the reader to notice these particular traits and to draw his attention to the similar traits which will enable him to see them as the essential characteristics of the writer's genius.

If the critic has felt this, and has helped others to feel it, his duties are more or less fulfilled. If he has not felt it, he can write all the books in the world about Ruskin – Ruskin the Man, the Writer, the Prophet, the Artist; The Range of His Activities, The Errors of His Doctrine; every edifice reaching the highest heights of excellence, perhaps – but he will have missed the point.

Ruskin in Venice

This man who has bathed the old cathedrals in more love and more joy than even the sun bestows when it adds its fleeting smile to their centuries-old beauty cannot, if we truly understand him, have been mistaken. But to what extent Ruskin's marvelous soul has faithfully reflected the world, and the touching and tempting forms in which deception and untruth have been able to slip, despite everything, into the heart of his intellectual sincerity, are matters we will never, perhaps, be given to know.

What I mean by these 'magnificent and tempting forms of deception and untruth' is that there is a kind of idolatry which no one has defined better than Ruskin himself, in the following passage from *Lectures on Art*:

> Such I conceive generally, though indeed with good arising out of it, for very great evil brings some good in its backward eddies – such I conceive to have been the deadly function of art in its ministry to what, whether in heathen or Christian lands, and whether in the pageantry of words, or colours, or fair forms, is truly, and in the deep sense, to be called idolatry – the serving with the best of our hearts and minds some dear and sad fantasy which we have made for ourselves, while we disobey the present call of the Master, who is not dead, and who is not fainting under His cross, but requiring us to take up ours.[1]

Now this very idolatry can, I think, be found at the deepest level of Ruskin's work, at the roots of his talent. Of course he

1. This sentence of Ruskin, I would add, applies better to idolatry as I understand it, taken out of context in this way, than to what it originally refers to in *Lectures on Art*.

never lets it completely overlay (even as an embellishment), immobilise, paralyse, and finally kill his intellectual and moral sincerity. In every line of his work, just as at every moment of his life, we can sense the need for sincerity fighting against idolatry, proclaiming its vanity, and humbling beauty before duty, even unaesthetic duty. I will not here draw examples from his life (a life which was not aesthetic first and moral afterwards, like that of a Racine, a Tolstoy, a Maeterlinck, but one in which morality asserted its rights from the beginning, even at the heart of the aesthetic – if perhaps without ever freeing itself from the aesthetic as completely as it did in the lives of the Masters I have just named). Ruskin's life is well known, and there is no need for me to recall its stages, from the first scruples he felt about drinking tea while looking at Titians to the moment when, having squandered on social and philanthropic works the fortune of five million his father had left him, he decided to sell his Turners. But there is a dilettantism more inward than the dilettantism of action which Ruskin overcame, and the true battle between his idolatry and his sincerity was played out not at certain hours of his life, not on certain pages of his books, but at every moment, in those deep, secret realms, almost unknown to ourselves, where our personality receives the images from our imagination, the ideas from our intelligence, and the words from our memory, and where it asserts itself in the continual choices it has to make among those images, ideas, words – where it incessantly rolls the dice so to speak of our moral and spiritual life. It seems to me that in those realms Ruskin never ceases to commit the sin of idolatry, and at the very moment when he preaches sincerity he lacks it himself, not in what he says but in how he says it. The doctrines he professed were moral doctrines, not aesthetic doctrines, but he chose them for their beauty, and since he did not want to present them as beautiful, rather as true, he was obliged to deceive himself about the nature of the reasons that had led him to adopt them. From this obligation arose a compromise of the conscience so incessant

that immoral doctrines, sincerely professed, may well have
been less dangerous to the integrity of his spirit than these
moral doctrines affirmed in a less than absolutely sincere way,
dictated as they were by an unacknowledged aesthetic preference. Such a sin was committed constantly, in every choice he
made – every explication of a fact, every appreciation of a work
of art, down to every word he used – and it ended up giving
a deceitful slant to the spirit that succumbed so ceaselessly
to this sin. So that the reader might better judge the kind of
optical illusion that a page of Ruskin is for us all, and evidently
was for Ruskin himself as well, I would like to quote here one
of the passages of his that I find most beautiful, where nevertheless this weakness is most glaring. We will see that if the
beauty of the page is *theoretically* subordinated to moral feeling
and to truth (that is, on the surface – since the content of
a writer's ideas is always superficial, and the form of his ideas
is their true reality), *in reality* the truth and the moral feeling
of the passage are subordinated to the aesthetic sentiment, and
moreover to an aesthetic sentiment somewhat falsified by these
perpetual compromises. The passage concerns the causes for
the decline of Venice:

Not in the wantonness of wealth, not in vain ministry to
the desire of the eyes or pride of life, were those marbles
hewn into transparent strength, and those arches arrayed
in the colours of the iris. There is a message written in the
dyes of them, that once was written in blood; and a sound
in the echoes of their vaults, that one day shall fill the
vault of heaven–' He shall return to do judgment and
justice.' [Gen. 18:19 – M.P.] The strength of Venice was
given her, so long as she remembered this; her destruction
found her when she had forgotten this; and it found her
irrevocably, because she forgot it without excuse. Never
had city a more glorious Bible. Among the nations of the
North, a rude and shadowy sculpture filled their temples

with confused and hardly legible imagery; but, for her, the skill and treasures of the East had gilded every letter, and illuminated every page, till the Book-Temple shone from afar off like the star of the Magi. In other cities, the meetings of the people were often in places withdrawn from religious association, subject to violence and to change; and on the grass of the dangerous rampart, and in the dust of the troubled street, there were deeds done and counsels taken, which, if we cannot justify, we may sometimes forgive. But the sins of Venice, whether in her palace or in her piazza, were done with the Bible at her right hand. The walls on which its testimony was written were separated but by a few inches of marble from those which guarded the secrets of her councils, or confined the victims of her policy. And when in her last hours she threw off all shame and restraint, and the great square of the city became filled with the madness of the whole earth, be it remembered how much her sin was greater, because it was done in the face of the House of God, burning with the letters of His Law.

Mountebank and masquer laughed their laugh, and went their way; and a silence has followed them, not unforetold; for amidst them all, through century after century of gathering vanity and fostering guilt, that white dome of St Mark's had uttered in the dead ear of Venice, 'Know thou, that for all these things God will bring thee into judgment.'[2]

Now if Ruskin had been entirely sincere with himself, he would not have thought that the crimes of the Venetians were harder to excuse than those of other men, and more severely punished, simply because the Venetians possessed a church of

2. *The Stones of Venice* I.IV.71. – The final verse is taken from Ecclesiastes (12:9).

many-coloured marble instead of a limestone cathedral, because the Doge's Palace was next to St Mark's instead of at the other end of the city, and because the Biblical passages in Byzantine churches were not only illustrated as they are in the sculpture of Northern churches, but also accompanied on the mosaics by letters forming a quotation from the Gospel or the prophecies. It is nonetheless true, however, that this passage from *The Stones of Venice* is one of great beauty, even though it may be difficult to analyse the reasons for this beauty.

The beauty seems to rest on something false, and we hesitate to give into it. Yet at the same time we must grant it a certain truth. There is, properly speaking, no beauty that is altogether false, because aesthetic pleasure is precisely that which accompanies the discovery of a truth. Just what order of truth the keen, quick aesthetic pleasure one takes in reading a passage like this may correspond to – that is what it is hard to say. The passage is mysterious, full of images at once beautiful and religious, like that same St Mark's Church, where all the characters of the Old and New Testaments appear against the background of a kind of splendid darkness and scintillating brilliance. I remember reading this page for the first time in St Mark's itself, during an hour of rain and darkness when the mosaics shone solely with their own material light, an inward, terrestrial, ancient gold into which the Venetian sun that sets even the angels atop the campaniles on fire mingled nothing of itself; the emotion I felt reading it there, among all these angels shining in their dark surroundings, was very great and yet not, perhaps, very pure. Just as the joy of seeing the beautiful, mysterious figures was heightened, but also tainted, by the somewhat academic pleasure I felt when I understood the texts in Byzantine letters visible alongside their haloed brows, so likewise the beauty of Ruskin's images was deepened but also corrupted by the pride of referring to the sacred text. A kind of egotistical return to oneself is inevitable in these joys, where art and erudition mingle and aesthetic pleasure may become more acute but cannot also remain as pure. Perhaps this page of *The Stones of Venice* – which, like St Mark's, had biblical quotations inscribed right next to its images in the mosaic of its dazzling, penumbral style – perhaps it was beautiful above all because it gave me the exact same adulterated pleasures I had felt in the Byzantine church. And was the page not also like the mosaics of St Mark's in another way too? Both intended to instruct, and set little store by their artistic beauty. Yet today they give us nothing but pleasure. The pleasure their didacticism gives the scholar is a selfish one, whereas the pleasure their beauty gives the artist is the most dis-interested – a beauty disdained, even unknown, by those whose only goal was to teach the people, who merely gave them a little beauty in addition.

On the last page, truly sublime, of *The Bible of Amiens*, the phrase 'if you would care for the promise to you' is an example of the same kind. Or when Ruskin, again in *The Bible of Amiens* (III.27), ends the section on Egypt by saying that 'She was the Tutress of Moses; and the Hostess of Christ', we may allow him the Tutress of Moses, for to educate requires certain virtues. But having been *the Hostess* of Christ – even if it adds to the beauty of the sentence, is it truly reasonable to include this claim in a judgment motivated solely by the virtues of Egypt?

It is with my most cherished aesthetic impressions that I have tried to wrestle here, pushing intellectual sincerity to its cruelest outermost limits. Need I add that, despite expressing this general reservation, in a *universal* sense and less about Ruskin's works than about the essential nature of their inspiration and the quality of their beauty, he nevertheless remains for me one of the greatest writers of all time and all countries? In him, as a particularly amenable 'subject', I have tried to grasp an essential frailty of the human spirit, not denounce a flaw in Ruskin personally.

I have had to descend to the depths of myself to grasp even the trace of this idolatry, and to study its nature and the some-what artificial element it mixes into the most vibrant literary pleasures which Ruskin gives us, since I am now 'used to' Ruskin. But the idolatry must have shocked me quite often when I was starting to love his books, before I closed my eyes little by little to their flaws, as one does whenever one falls in love. Love for another living creature often has a sordid origin which is later purified. A man makes the acquaintance of a woman because she can help him attain a goal that has nothing to do with her; then, after he has gotten to know her, he loves her for her own sake and does not hesitate for a moment to sacrifice to her the goal she was only there in the first place to help him reach. In the same way, my love for Ruskin's books was blended at first with something of selfish interest: the pleasure of the intellectual profit I intended to draw from them. Certainly, while I read the first few pages and felt their power and charm, I forced myself not to resist them, not to argue too much within myself, because I sensed that if the charm of Ruskin's thought could one day extend for me over everything it touched – if, in a word, I would one day be completely taken with it – then the world would be enriched with everything I had not known before: the Gothic cathedrals, the countless English and Italian paintings which had not yet awakened in me the desire without which there is never true knowledge. For Ruskin's ideas are not like Emerson's, for example, which can be entirely contained in a book, that is, in an abstract thing, a pure sign of themselves. The object to which an idea like Ruskin's refers, from which it cannot be separated, is not immaterial: it is scattered here and there across the surface of the earth. You have to go in search of it where it can be found – in Pisa, in Florence, in Venice, at the National Gallery, in Rouen, in Amiens, in the mountains of Switzerland. An idea like that, which has as its object something other than itself, which has realised itself in space, is no longer free and infinite thought, but limited, subjected, incarnate in bodies sculpted of marble, in cloud-covered mountains, in painted countenances, and it may well be less godlike than pure thought but it makes the world more beautiful to us, or at least makes certain parts of the world, certain named individual parts, more beautiful to us, because it has touched them and because it has initiated us into them by making us, if we want to understand it, love them.

That is in fact what happened: all at once the world regained infinite value in my eyes. And my admiration for Ruskin gave such importance to the things he had made me love that they seemed charged with a value literally greater than that of life itself. At a time when I thought that my days were nearing their end, I set out for Venice so that I could, before I died, approach and touch and see incarnated in the rosy palaces, crumbling but nevertheless still standing, Ruskin's ideas about the domestic architecture of the Middle Ages. What importance, what reality, could a city like Venice have – unique, fixed in time and localised in space – in the eyes of someone so soon to depart from this earth? How could the theories of domestic architecture that I could study and verify there in these living examples be among those 'truths which are more powerful than death, which keep us from fearing death and almost make us love it'?[3] It is the power of genius to make us love a beauty we feel to be more real than we are, in things which are in others' eyes as particular and as perishable as ourselves.

3. Renan.

Servitude and Freedom

Second-rate minds generally think that to let yourself be guided by the books you admire detracts from the independence of your faculty of judgment. 'What should it matter to you what Ruskin feels: feel for yourself!' Such opinions rest on a psychological mistake which can be disposed of properly by anyone who has accepted this type of spiritual discipline and felt their powers of comprehension and feeling immeasurably increased thereby, and their critical faculties not paralysed in the slightest. In such circumstances we are, quite simply, in a state of grace, when all of our faculties are invigorated, our critical sense as much as the rest. So too, this voluntary servitude is the beginning of freedom. There is no better way to discover what you feel than to try to re-create in yourself what a master has felt. In this profound effort, it is our own thoughts that we bring to light by means of his. Our life is free but only because it has a purpose – it has been a long time since anyone believed in the sophistry of freedom through indifference, and it is an equally naive sophistry that writers succumb to unawares when they try to empty their minds at every moment, unburden themselves of every external influence, to ensure that they remain their own unique selves. In reality, the only times when we truly have all our intellectual and spiritual powers at our disposal are the times when we do not think we are acting independently, when we do not arbitrarily choose the goal toward which we direct our efforts. The novelist's theme, the poet's vision, the philosopher's truth forces itself upon him in an almost necessary way, external to his own mind as it were. And it is precisely by subordinating his spirit to the task of expressing this vision, of approaching this truth, that the artist becomes truly himself.

Resurrection

Ruskin's medieval studies, together with his belief in the goodness of faith, confirmed his belief in the necessity of free, joyful, and personal labour without mechanical intervention. You will perceive this best if I transcribe here a passage very characteristic of Ruskin. He is talking about a little figure a few inches high, lost in a crowd of hundreds of tiny figures at the Portal of the Booksellers of the Rouen cathedral:

> The fellow is vexed and puzzled in his malice; and his hand is pressed hard on his cheek bone, and the flesh of the cheek is *wrinkled* under the eye by the pressure. The whole, indeed, looks wretchedly coarse, when it is seen on a scale in which it is naturally compared with delicate figure etchings; but considering it as a mere filling of an interstice on the outside of a cathedral gate, and as one of more than three hundred (for in my estimate I did not include the outer pedestals), it proves very noble vitality in the art of the time.
>
> We have certain work to do for our bread, and that is to be done strenuously; other work to do for our delight, and that is to be done heartily: neither is to be done by halves and shifts, but with a will; and what is not worth this effort is not to be done at all. Perhaps all that we have to do is meant for nothing more than an exercise of the heart and of the will, and is useless in itself; but, at all events, the little use it has may well be spared if it is not worth putting our hands and our strength to. It does not become our immortality to take an ease inconsistent with its authority, nor to suffer any instruments with which it can dispense, to come between it and the things it rules: and he who would form the creations of his own mind by any other instrument than his own hand, would also, if he might,

give grinding organs to Heaven's angels, to make their music easier. There is dreaming enough, and earthiness enough, and sensuality enough in human existence, without our turning the few glowing moments of it into mechanism; and since our life must at the best be but a vapour that appears for a little time and then vanishes away, let it at least appear as a cloud in the height of Heaven, not as the thick darkness that broods over the blast of the Furnace, and rolling of the Wheel.

I confess that when I reread this page, upon Ruskin's death, I was seized by the desire to see the little fellow he describes. And so I went to Rouen, as if obeying a last wish, as if Ruskin, dying, had in a sense bequeathed this poor creature to his readers. Ruskin had given him life by speaking of him, and the creature had just lost forever, without knowing it, someone who had done as much for him as his original sculptor. But when I came to the immense cathedral and stood in front of the portal where the saints up above were warming themselves in the sun, from the galleries where the kings radiated out up to the supreme heights of stone that I had thought were uninhabited, with here a sculpted hermit, living in isolation and letting birds sojourn on his forehead, there a cenacle of apostles, listening to the message of an angel who had landed nearby and refolded his wings beneath a flock of pigeons who had just opened theirs, not far off a figure on whose back a child had just landed, turning his head in an abrupt, age-old gesture; when I saw all these denizens in stone of the mystical city, arrayed before the cathedral entrance or leaning over the balconies of its towers, breathing in the sun or the morning shadows, I knew it would be impossible to find a single figure a few inches high in this superhuman multitude. I nevertheless went up to the Portal of the Booksellers. But how could I recognise the one little fellow among the hundreds of others? Suddenly the talented and promising young sculptor I was with, Louise Yeatman, said: 'Here's one that looks like it.' We look a little lower and – there he is. He is less than four inches tall, a little crumbled, but the gaze is still the same: the stone has preserved the indentation which put the pupil in relief and gave him the expression by which I recognise him. There, among thousands of other figures, an artist dead for centuries has left this little fellow who dies a little each day, and who for a very long time has been altogether dead, lost in the crowd of others, forever. But this artist set him there in his place and one day a man for whom there is no death, for whom there is no materialist infinity, no forgetting, a man who casts off the nothingness that oppresses us in order to pursue the goals which rule his life, goals so numerous that he cannot attain them all while we ourselves seem not to have even one – this man arrives and among these waves of stone whose every eroded, foamy crest seems to resemble every other, he sees all of the laws of life, all the thoughts of the soul, and he calls them by their true name and he says: 'Look. It is this, it is that.' As though on the Day of Judgment, depicted in stone not far away, he lets his words be heard like the trumpet of the archangel and he says: 'Those who have lived shall live, matter is nothing.' And in fact, like the dead – whom the nearby tympanum shows reawakened at the blast of the archangel's trumpet, arisen, having taken on their bodies again, recognisable, alive – the little fellow here has been brought back to life, has found his gaze once more, and the Judge has said: 'You have lived, you shall live again.' As for him, he is not an immortal judge, his body will die, but what does it matter! As though dying were not in fact his destiny, he accomplishes his immortal task, caring nothing about the size of the thing that occupies his time; with only one human life to live, he spends several of its days in front of one among ten thousand figures on a single church. He drew it. For him it corresponded to the ideas which stirred in his brain, irrespective of the approach of old age. He drew it, he spoke of it. And the innocuous, even monstrous little figure would be brought back to life, against all hope, from a death which seems even more final than other deaths – disappearance into numerical infinity under the leveling of likeness – but from which genius means to save us too. We cannot help but be moved by finding the little fellow there. He seems to live and see us, or rather he seems to have been taken by death in the very moment of this gaze, like the Pompeiians interrupted forever in mid-gesture. It is, in fact, the thought of the sculptor, seized here mid-gesture by the immobility of stone. I was touched to recapture it here; it means that nothing dies which has ever lived, neither the thought of the sculptor nor the thought of John Ruskin.

Encountering the little figure here – so necessary to Ruskin that he devoted one of the very few illustrations in his book to it, for it was a living and lasting part of his thought; and pleasing to us, because his thought is necessary to us, a guide to our own now that we, on our own path, have encountered it – we feel ourselves to be in a state of mind closer to that of the artists who made the sculptures of the Last Judgment on the tympanum and who thought that the individual, that which is most particular to a person or an intention, does not die but remains in the memory of God and will be resurrected. Who is right, the gravedigger or Hamlet, when one sees only a skull before him while the other calls up a fancy of his imagination? Science may say the gravedigger, but science has failed to take account of Shakespeare, who will make the memory of this fancy outlast even the dust of the skull. At the summons of the angel, all of the dead still find themselves there in their place, where we thought them long ago turned to dust. At the summons of Ruskin, we see the smallest figure, framing a miniscule quatre-foil, resurrected in its body, looking at us with the same gaze that seems to be held in no more than a millimetre of stone. It is true, poor little monster, that I would not have been able to find you among the millions of stones in all the cities, to pick out your shape, to recapture your personality, to speak your name, to bring you back to life. But that is not because infinity, number, nothingness, the things that oppress us, are too strong; it is because my own mind is too weak. Granted, there is nothing truly beautiful about you. Your poor little face, which I would never have noticed, does not have a particularly interesting expression, although it does have, of course, like everyone's, an expression that no one else has ever had. But since you were alive enough to keep looking with that same sidelong gaze, so that Ruskin noticed you and, having spoken your name, made it possible for his reader to recognise you, are you still alive enough? Are you loved enough? One cannot help but think of you with affection, however ugly you may seem, because you are a living creature, because, down through the long centuries, you were dead without hope of resurrection and because you have been resurrected. And one of these days maybe someone else will go to find you at your portal, will look with affection upon your wretched sloping resurrected face, because only what has gone forth from one mind can one day captivate another mind which has in turn enchanted our own. You were right to remain there, unnoticed, crumbling. You could expect nothing from matter, in which you were merely nothingness, but the little ones have nothing to fear, nor do the dead. For sometimes the Spirit visits the earth; in its wake the dead arise, the little for-gotten figures regain their gaze and capture the regard of the living who, for them, abandon the living who do not live and go in search of life only where the Spirit has revealed it to them, in the stones which are already dust and yet still of the mind.

Biographical note

Marcel Proust was born in Paris in July 1871. His mother came from a well-off Jewish family, and his father was a doctor. In the 1890s, Proust began to move in fashionable Parisian circles; under the patronage of Anatole France, he published his first book, *Les Plaisirs et les Jours (The Pleasures and the Days)*, in 1896. After this, Proust devoted several years to translating and annotating the works of the art historian John Ruskin. He published a number of articles on Ruskin, as well as two translations: *The Bible of Amiens* in 1904 and *Sesame and Lilies* in 1906.

During the summer of 1909 Proust developed an essay entitled '*Contre Sainte Beuve*' into a novel which he would continue to write for the rest of his life. In May of 1913 he decided to call it *A la recherche du temps perdu (In Search of Lost Time)*.

The first part, *Du Côté de chez Swann*, was published in November 1913. War delayed *A l'ombre des jeunes filles en fleurs* until June 1919, but it won the Prix Goncourt in December of that year. Proust continued working on the novel for the last three years of his life, and during this time, three more volumes appeared: *Le côté de Guermantes I* (October 1920), *Le côté de Guermantes II – Sodome et Gomorrhe I* (May 1921), *Sodome et Gomorrhe II* (April 1922).

Proust died of pneumonia on 18th November 1922. The remaining volumes of his novel, which he had finished but not completely revised, were published by his brother Robert, with the help of Jacques Rivière and Jean Paulhan, directors of La Nouvelle Revue Française.

Damion Searls is an award-winning translator of writers including Rilke, Ingeborg Bachmann, Jon Fosse, Hans Keilson and Robert Walser. He is also the author of *What We Were Doing and Where We Were Going* (stories) and the editor of Henry David Thoreau's *The Journal: 1837–1861*.

HESPERUS PRESS

Hesperus Press is committed to bringing near what is far – far both in space and time. Works written by the greatest authors, and unjustly neglected or simply little known in the English-speaking world, are made accessible through new translations and a completely fresh editorial approach. Through these classic works, the reader is introduced to the greatest writers from all times and all cultures.

For more information on Hesperus Press, please visit our website: **www.hesperuspress.com**